Raising Nathan

"Every life has a story"

Christine E. Staple-Ebanks

Chief Editors

Stephanie Hornett, Red Raygun Ltd, Bridport, UK
Yvonne O. Coke, Kingston, Jamaica W.I.

Contributing Editors

David W. Thomforde, Occupational Therapist, Michigan,
    USA, UN Volunteer
Suraj Sharma, UN Youth Volunteer

With special thanks to the UNV Online Volunteering Service

Raising Nathan

Christine E. Staple-Ebanks

Cover and Interior Design/Layout: © 2015 Michael Talbot

ISBN number – 10:069252200X
ISBN number – 13:978-0-692-52200-4

Library of Congress Cataloging-in-Publication Data.

With love to my son Nathan, who came to me as a gift from God to release me into a deeper love and higher purpose, and who has opened my heart and eyes to see every human being as a unique expression of God in the earth.

-

To my husband Robert, who is my best friend, my encourager, and my greatest cheerleader. Thank you for choosing to be the wind beneath my wings.

-

To my daughters Adrianne and Jordanne, and my son Ryan who continue to be a source of joy and inspiration, helping me to share this story with authenticity.

-

With thanks, love and deep appreciation to my mother Aleith Davis, who as a single parent raised my five siblings and I, and who taught us to be strong, courageous, and the love of God. My sister Jennifer Staple-Gowdie who has been my shoulder to lean on throughout the years, my faithful companion on those far away trips and a second mom to my children, thank you.

-

In loving memory of Nathan's paternal grandmother, *Ivy Rita Ebanks.*

CONTENTS

Foreword

So what's the big deal about raising Nathan? It's a big, big deal alright! Big enough for the American government to recognize the singular work being done by this family to transform the thinking of a nation on the subject of disability inclusion. Raising Nathan is a book which Christine Staple-Ebanks was commissioned by God to write through her son, Nathan. Nathan is the perfect evangelist for the cause of people with disabilities. He is armed with real weapons of disarmament, chief of which his mother calls "his killer smile", which he has learned to skill-fully unleash. When unleashed upon unsuspecting victims, Nathan's heart-warming smile arrests and renders them powerless to turn away without a positive response.

His eyes, which tell a tale of their own and puts Nathan in a place above human knowledge and understanding of the real need of the human soul for unfettered love which compels to lay aside every weight, is a gift of God to Jamaica in her quest to fulfill the nation's purpose. He is here to point us to and to challenge the nation of

Jamaica to keep our pledge: *"Before God and all mankind..."* to *"...play our part in advancing the welfare of the whole human race."* Nowhere is Jamaica more challenged by this than in the way we raise our children, either enabling those with a disability or disabling of the able-bodied. The words of warning from the author of our nation's national anthem and pledge come to mind: *"There is a war going on for Jamaica. It is a war of... child care against child abuse."* He continues: *"...Stop! You are on the wrong road, right about turn and march. March away from that destination which will mean ruin and an abuse of Independence which will result in the destruction of our nation."* (Perspectives from the Jamaican MAP pp.53;54).

This account of raising a child with a severe disability to fulfill his own God-given purpose, is one which brought me to tears where I could not continue the editing for hours or days. I laughed, I groaned, I cried, but at the end I felt the triumph of Nathan and his family over the circumstances of his disability as we all come to realize that indeed, Nathan is a gift and so is this account of this amazing journey.

Yvonne O. Coke

Author

Acknowledgements

Thanks to the Lord God Almighty for the wonderful gift of Nathan to me, my family, my nation and the world. Thanks to my husband and my best friend Robert for sharing his life, love and our family, and for being such an amazing father to our children. To my mother Aleith Davis, sister Jennifer, friends Wendean Bryan and Dawn Coombs (deceased) and others who have journeyed with us from the start.

Thanks to Senta Greene a remarkable woman, mother, educator and child life specialist and my mentor for the past eight years. Thanks to Karaine Smith-Holness and Simone Fisher-Sobers, and Tara Caroll Malphrus, who are my cheerleaders and strong advocates. Thanks to the editors-in-chief, Stephanie Hornett and Yvonne O. Coke; contributing editor, David Thomforde; Michael Talbot for the cover design and layout and to Dr Kay Ann Bookall for supporting this project.

Thanks to Rene Lambert for continuing to inspire me with her courage as she navigates the education system as a young woman gifted with cerebral palsy, and to Michelle Whervin-Maxwell, a phenomenal teacher who continues to challenge herself to help Nathan succeed in school. Thanks to all families with children with cerebral palsy and other disabilities who have shared their, knowledge, stories and courage with us.

I dedicate this work to the memory of my friend Dawn Coombs, who helped me to change my vantage point from seeing my son's disability to seeing the child who was masked behind the disability.

Lastly, but by no means least, I wish to give a very special thanks to Elaine Wint and Dr. Fay E. Brown, who have mentored me in parts of my journey and are especially instrumental in me writing this book. To my friend Curline Beckford for her prayers and support in more ways than I can count, and to my friends of UN Online Volunteers and the UNV Online Volunteer Service for supporting this project through to printing.

Preface

"Every life has a story." When a friend shared this with me a few years ago as we discussed a particular project we were working on, it struck me as profound. I am fairly certain that this was not an original idea, but when she said it her words jolted me like a bolt of lightning. If I were to describe my mental state at that moment, I would liken it to a swirling vortex with my life experiences and fragments of my beliefs whirling around since the day I heard the doctor say, "Mom, there is something wrong with your child." That day was eight years before and the 'child' was not yet born – I was only five months pregnant.

My friend's voice rapidly faded into the background as I was caught up in her matter-of-fact statement. It felt like the control on the reigns of my life had slipped when I learned I was pregnant with my fourth child and the subsequent onslaught of negativism started – the identification of a birth defect in my unborn baby, my 'sentence' of staying in hospital during the last two months of the pregnancy, the trauma of the delivery, my baby's destiny-altering surgery, his hospitalization for the first 24 days of his life, the diagnosis of a major disability and learning how to cope... it was all too much and I was shock-weary.

I had been asking God for answers... Why? Why me? Why my child? Why this condition? What is it? What am I to do? How will I cope? Why? Why? Why? So my friend's seemingly simple statement was both an answer and a message. The effect of the words was the start of a change in the course of the whirlwind that was my thinking up until then. Have you ever had the feeling of being lost? Powerless? Helpless? Spent? An unshakable feeling like you are caught up in someone else's nightmare and can't wake up? Or someone made really bad decisions on your behalf and didn't bother to tell you, and are no where to be found?

And then you receive a *word* that quickens you and a positive bolt of energy is shot like an arrow into the negative charge that was life up to that point. The words from my friend, "Every life has a story," became a catalyst that day which gave me a different perspective... a new way of looking at a 'bad' situation, and turned it all around.

Until she made that statement, I hadn't thought about my life as telling a story... but the more I pondered the statement, the more I became convicted of this simple truth. This statement change my life. As I reflect on the experience I am about to share through the pages of this book, I can now see how my friend's analogy has shifted my focus and given me a new set of lens through which to view my experiences. With the passage of time, I can see the core elements of the story... my story... the characters, themes, setting, plot, conflict, resolution and the denouement...

So sit back and enjoy the journey. May you be inspired. Empowered. Encouraged. Motivated.

This is my story – this is Nathan's story.

Heaven's Very Special Child

A meeting was held quite far from Earth!
It's time again for another birth.
Said the Angels to the LORD above,
This Special Child will need much love.

His progress may be very slow,
Accomplishments he may not show.
And he'll require extra care
From the folks he meets down there.

He may not run or laugh or play,
His thoughts may seem quite far away.
In many ways he won't adapt,
And he'll be known as handicapped.

So let's be careful where he's sent,
We want his life to be content.
Please LORD, find the parents who
Will do a special job for you.

They will not realize right away
The leading role they're asked to play.
But with this child sent from above
Comes stronger faith and richer love.

And soon they'll know the privilege given
In caring for their gift from Heaven.
Their precious charge, so meek and mild,
Is HEAVEN'S VERY SPECIAL CHILD.

by **Edna Massionilla**

Chapter 1
Life Interrupted

I remember the day like it was yesterday. It is indelibly etched upon my very soul. The silence in the consultation room was deafening as I sat facing my OB/GYN,[1] looking at the top of his bent head. He seemed oblivious to my presence as he sat staring intently at the ultrasound scan of my very pregnant tummy, which he had taken moments before. He was muttering to himself as if in wonder. "This can't be right," he said to himself, "How could I not have noticed this before?" I felt the cold fingers of fear travelling up my spine. What was it he saw? Why did he not see it before now? What does this all mean? Questions assaulted my brain as I struggled to remain calm. This was my fourth pregnancy after all, and I had never experienced any complications before, so what could go wrong? As I waited for the doctor to speak to me I gave myself a pep talk, but all the while I felt a sick certainty in the pit of my stomach that there was something very wrong with my unborn child.

Raising Nathan

I was so wrapped up in myself and my own thoughts that I forgot that my husband, Robert, was sitting in the chair next to me, and I didn't have to go through this alone. Robert must have sat motionless because I have no recollection of him being there. I was frightened out of my wits, caught up in the intensity of the moment, unaware that Robert was in a similar position to me. In fact, during that specific part of the day, I can't recall him being with me at all even though it was he who drove us there and drove us home afterwards! When I now recall how the day started and ended, I realize that he had been there every step of the way.

As I sat waiting for my doctor to speak, the question flooded my consciousness, "How can an atmosphere change so rapidly?" I could barely breathe. I couldn't imagine what I was about to face, and I wasn't sure that I wanted to know. If only I could reverse time and start the day all over again. Instead I felt alone, trapped in my own mind as my thoughts raced out of control, with only the sound of my laboured breathing, the doctor's muttering and the tick-tock of the clock hanging on the wall for company. I was in a bubble sealed off from the outside world. The wait for the

doctor to speak seemed interminable as I struggled
to remain calm, tension and fear creeping upwards
steadily and insistently from the pit of my stomach.
I wished he would say something, and I wished he
wouldn't.

Just moments before we were laughing! I was wailing
over my poor swollen feet, my never-ending hunger
pangs and my growing midriff as I lost my waistline.
We had been joking together as I recounted how a
conference call at work overran the time earlier in
the week, cutting into my 'baby-fixed' eating time and
making me cry.

It was December 2003, and this was my last prenatal
visit before the Christmas holidays. Ever since I was
a little girl, I have always loved this time of year – the
Christmas breeze, the cheerful atmosphere and the
decorations – somehow it feels like people are happier
around this special holiday. Christmas was even more
special when I became a mother. No matter what has
transpired during the year, my mood begins to perk
up around October as I wait with childlike anticipation
for the yuletide season to arrive. I had no idea that my
life was about to undergo a major overhaul on this

Raising Nathan

fateful day in my favourite month. All my previous prenatal visits had gone well and I considered myself an expert having already had three successful pregnancies. The thought that something could go wrong never entered my mind – but I was languishing in a false sense of security.

Robert and my doctor were in stitches when suddenly the doctor became still and quiet. He was staring intently at the ultrasound screen, a perplexed look on his face. This cannot be good, I thought. Following his cue, I too fell quiet. He kept running the scan probe over my enlarged tummy as if he was trying to see something specific from different angles. I tried to re-engage him in conversation, but he had become uncommunicative and I sensed his alarm. I gave up trying to talk to him and waited for him to speak.

Finally after what seemed like an eternity, he looked up and without making eye contact told me I could get dressed, and left the cubicle. Dressing quickly I returned to sit by his desk, studying his face carefully trying to anticipate what he was getting ready to say. Inside I was screaming, "What's wrong with my baby?" But I could not utter the words. So I remained silent, my stomach in knots, I could feel the beginning of a headache. "How did I miss this? How could I not have seen it? It was so obvious!" said Dr Sideman.[2] He fell silent again and after a few moments, in my calmest voice, I asked, "Missed what Doctor? What is going on?"

I can't recall why Robert had accompanied me to see Dr Sideman. Having been pregnant three times before, although this one was a 'surprise', I saw no reason for him to leave work to attend my prenatal visits – he already had to leave work early for classes as he was studying towards a master's degree. But for whatever the reason, he had decided to accompany me that day. As we entered the doctor's office earlier that afternoon my biggest concern was whether we were going to have a baby boy or girl. We already had two daughters and a son – Adrianne was seven years old, followed by Ryan who was six, and baby Jordanne was three. As I waited for Dr Sideman to speak, I didn't know what to think or do. My mind flashed back to the months leading up to the pregnancy.

The pregnancy took me – us – by surprise. Life was hectic in our home but we had settled into a good routine. With three young children and the demands of our jobs – Robert in finance and mine as a market planning manager for a major company in Jamaica – having a new baby was not in our plans. I once heard that 'God does nothing without first warning us' and took it to heart. If truth be told, I had secretly harboured the idea of another baby, but I thought that perhaps when our three were grown, Robert and I would adopt a child. About a year previously I was sitting in Church listening to the annual Good Friday sermon, when as if in a vision I saw myself heavily pregnant. It was disconcerting and I wondered what it meant. After Church I told my sister about the vision and we had a good laugh as she said, "Chris, you woudda mus' dead if you get pregnant now!" I agreed, and as time passed I forgot all about it.

Just over a year later, the premonition became a reality! I knew deep down that I was pregnant, but refused to acknowledge it. I woke one morning feeling awful. It was not the same kind of feeling that I had with my earlier pregnancies, it was a low feeling like I was coming down with the flu. I felt like I had run a marathon the day before. My whole body ached, and I could hardly open my eyes. I was sluggish and just couldn't shake the fatigue that had descended upon me. I struggled through the morning routine, getting the children ready for school, wanting nothing more than to crawl back into bed to sleep. However I was in charge of organizing a major corporate event and had scheduled meetings and other appointments that day.

Despite my best efforts I arrived at work late, and after a few hours of trying to concentrate but not being able to focus I decided to follow my body, cancel my meetings and head back home and go to bed. With this decision now firmly made, it was as I was about to telephone my shared assistant, Rose-Marie, to ask her to reschedule my meetings, when I heard a small voice behind me say, "You are pregnant!" "What?" I asked swivelling in my chair to see who was there, only to find that I was alone in my semi-enclosed office. I returned to making the call and having done so, once again heard the same voice, even more firmly repeat the words, "You are pregnant!" I knew there would be no one there, but checked anyway! Feeling vaguely alarmed, I chalked it up to my mind playing tricks on me. I must be sicker than I thought, I said to myself.

As I got up from my chair to leave, I felt like thousands of tiny spikes were pricking me all over. It felt like pins and needles, not only in my fingers and toes, but over my entire body. I sat back in the chair, now very alarmed. "What is going on with me?" I thought. Being pregnant was still not something I was willing to consider. At that moment, Rose-Marie pushed her head into my office to speak to me. She took one look at my face and said "Oh no Chris, you don't look so good! Are you okay?" I steadied myself before replying that I was not, and that I would be heading home shortly. As I spoke, the voice in my head said, "Stop by the pharmacy on your way home to buy a pregnancy kit. You are pregnant." There was no escaping the thought, "Could I really be pregnant?"

Before I could get up again, Karyn, the project decorator called. I had forgotten to cancel our meeting but we agreed to reschedule when I told her that I was unwell. I also reluctantly agreed to collect a package on her behalf and meet her at the pharmacy where I planned to stop. I decided I would hand the package over to her in the car park and maintain my privacy while making my clandestine purchase. I wasn't ready to tell anyone that I might be pregnant. I wasn't even ready to share the news with myself.

It was just after midday when I arrived at the pharmacy and Karyn was already there. I saw her car immediately when I pulled into the car park. I was a little dismayed and anxious that I had missed the opportunity to make my purchase before her arrival, however, I parked alongside her car ready to make the handover. Breathing a sigh of relief I was able to give her a genuine smile as I told myself that things were not going to be as bad as I had anticipated.

We exchanged a hug and pleasantries, but to my dismay she became very chatty and didn't seem in any hurry to leave! I kept looking at my watch hoping she would take the hint that I needed to go. Whether by design or omission she didn't pick up on my clues and so after a brief pause, I told her I had to run. As I turned to go she asked whether I was going into the pharmacy. I reluctantly said, "Yes," and my heart fell when she responded that she too had to pick up a few items there, and started walking with me. I was torn as to whether I should make the purchase as planned or whether I should go to another pharmacy where I could be alone. To my relief, when we got to the door, Karyn turned towards the adjoining supermarket. We said our goodbyes and I entered the pharmacy... alone.

I headed straight to the shelf which stocked the pregnancy kits and selected one. I was pleased that there was only one other customer in line at the cashier. As I reached into my handbag for my purse I saw it in my mind's eye, sitting on the kitchen counter at home where I had put it that morning after giving lunch money to my children. The purse held my driver's licence, cash, debit and credit cards – I had no money on me! I rummaged around in my handbag for a few seconds to make sure that it wasn't my imagination, but came up empty-handed. As I looked up at the cashier, I heard Karyn right behind me asking if I had forgotten my purse. Before I could reply, she stepped forward, placed some money on the counter and said, "Here, let me pay for that for you." I felt like a kid whose hand was caught in the cookie jar! I stood there speechless while she paid the cashier, collected my package and turned and handed it to me. Seeing how flustered I was, she immediately apologized for possibly overstepping the boundaries as it was then that she realized that I must have wanted privacy. She explained that she had come into the pharmacy to talk to someone and noticed my dilemma. Taking the package, I found my voice sufficiently to mutter an embarrassed, "Thank you," before heading to the exit.

Much to my chagrin, she followed me and as we left the pharmacy asked if I thought I might be pregnant. Without waiting for an answer she said she would give her 'eye teeth' to be in my shoes, explaining that she was well over 40 years old and had been trying to conceive for the past five years. She went on to share that she and her husband had not had children together, and that her children, who were all grown up were from an earlier marriage. She said that she was sure that her husband loved her children, but she felt that he wanted a child of his own. With sad eyes she told me she was fearful that she would lose him if she couldn't give him a child. I did not know what to say.

We had paused outside the door of the pharmacy as she spoke. We stood in silence for a few minutes, my head knew I should say something encouraging to her, but my heart was fixed on my own dilemma. "I am very happy for you," she said after a short silence. "I do hope you are pregnant." As she turned to walk away, I heard the words, "Enjoy the gift." With that, she was gone. As I watched her retreating back, I pondered whether I should spend 15 to 20 minutes driving home to take the test, or stop at either my sister's or brother's who both lived nearby. The decision was made after two phone calls. My sister was still at work but my brother, who lived two minutes away, was at home.

Michael was on his veranda when I arrived, and when I told him I needed to use the bathroom urgently he looked at me curiously. I closed the bathroom door behind me and leaned against it. Now that the moment had arrived, I was suddenly not sure what I wanted to do. I wasn't ready for what I might find out. What if the test was positive? What if it was negative? I had not committed to a decision on what I wanted from the test. I felt weak. After a few minutes, I pulled myself together and with a deep breath, took the test. What followed next was a shocker. Two vibrant pink lines and the word **POSITIVE** confirmed what I knew deep-down all along. I was pregnant!

Still, I still wondered, how could this be? A quick calculation revealed that I had conceived within the last three to five days. I must have been in the bathroom for a long time because Michael knocked gently on the door to ask if I was alright. I told him I was fine and would be out in a minute. It felt like the end of the world. "What am I going to do?" I thought to myself as I felt panic rising. "How could I face another pregnancy?" I had just barely got my body back in shape, after Jordanne. It got harder and harder each time to balance work, babies, young children and the gym. I felt a wave of weakness wash over me. I didn't know if I had the energy to go through the process of pregnancy, delivery, babyhood all over again. Realizing that I could not stay in my brother's bathroom forever, I stood up, washed my hands and face, straightened up, and opened the door and walked down the hall to the living room.

Michael was standing in the living room when I entered, looking a bit worried. He looked at my face and asked, "Everything is everything?" (meaning is everything all right?) I blurted out "I'm pregnant." To my annoyance, he started to chuckle, then broke out laughing outright. "I'm glad you find humour in this," I snapped at him. "No, it's not that," he replied. "It is just that if I had known you were going to do a pregnancy test in there, I would have told you not to and let you use the other bathroom, because no test has ever gone into that bathroom and come back negative!" I saw the irony as he and his wife at the time had two pregnancies in quick succession.

Raising Nathan

However, I was not able to appreciate the humour of his statement at the time, as my mind was on bigger things. I took my leave shortly after, and as I turned onto the main road I noted that as it was later in the afternoon, I was now in the height of the Friday evening traffic which was bumper to bumper. The drive home would take anywhere from an hour and a half to two hours. I felt slightly comforted, it gave me a chance to clear my head and organize my thoughts before I got home.

As I crawled along in the traffic, all I could think of was how was I going to break this news to Robert? Only a few days before, we were celebrating the fact that Jordanne, our youngest, had just graduated from training pants. How ironic! We had had three children in five years, being sleep deprived from the midnight feedings and all the other emergencies which are part and parcel of parenting young children. Furthermore, Robert was just a few courses away from completing his master's and he was delighted that after five years of getting the night shift with our children, including two years of studying at nights he was finally about to get his nights back. Robert is a very caring, thoughtful and loving husband, who in my and our children's estimation won father of the year hands down every time. But... I was still worried about how he was going to take the news. And with our three children in preparatory school, a new baby would certainly challenge our finances.

Raising Nathan

Chapter 2
The Seed of Hope

The traffic crawled along and I with it. When I finally pulled into our driveway it had grown dark. More than five hours had passed since I left the office and about two hours since learning that I was pregnant. I parked the car in our driveway and sat, gathering my composure. Robert and I were married in 1997. He is my best friend, sensitive and very supportive husband, warm, passionate, hands-on dad... my soul mate. We met in the second semester of our second year at the University of the West Indies, and by the end of the semester we had begun dating. It was a very romantic courtship. Unknown to us we stood out as a couple, and were even nominated 'Best Couple' for the Student Union's Valentine's Day Celebrations in 1993 – we weren't even aware we were in the running! Sometimes I bump into people who were on the university campus while we were there who remember me as one half of this 'lovely couple'. One even commented that she clapped for joy on seeing us with a baby chair on our back seat and realized that we had married and started a family.

But none of that mattered or entered my mind in this 'crisis'. I was worried about telling **my** husband that we were having another baby. I remembered when I had told him I was pregnant with Jordanne, he had stared blankly at me and asked, "How?" I had been so mad! How could one little word hurt me? But it had. I had conjured up this story that he would be thrilled with the news and would hug and kiss me. Instead all he said was "How?" I realized that his response was one of surprise. And after that initial shock he was wonderful. He was the perfect doting husband and overly protective father-to-be, who moved heaven and earth to get me a jar of pickles at midnight once during the pregnancy when I felt I would 'die' if I didn't get pickles! He found an open gas (petrol) station that had them in stock, and brought home a jar, looking like he had won the main prize. I took one bite of a pickle and couldn't even finish it! Robert ate the whole jar before going to bed. Yet here I was three years later, sitting in my car, afraid to go into my house and tell my husband that I was pregnant with our baby!

I whispered out loud, "Lord, how am I going to tell my husband that I am pregnant again? You know that we are barely keeping our heads above water, how on earth can we afford another child now? You were there when Robert said how he was looking forward to finally getting his nights back. So how do I go inside and tell him that a new baby is on its way?" Almost immediately I heard the same voice from earlier that day whisper, "This child is a gift from God. Tell Robert that this child is a gift from Me (God). His name is to mean 'Gift from God'. With this child you will prove who I am." In that moment I knew that I was carrying a child of purpose. I didn't know what it all meant, purpose for what, but somehow in that moment I knew that my child would be somehow special. I know that all children are special, and my three children before are all special in their unique way. But there was something about this baby... it was time to go inside and face Robert.

I entered our living room. Robert was lying on the couch and the children were playing in their rooms. His eyes opened and made a beeline for me in the wonderful and familiar way that would occur when-ever I entered a space where he was. I felt guilty for what I was about to tell him. I sat beside him and tried to smile. I think he knew intuitively what I was about to say, because he didn't seem shocked or perturbed when I told him I was pregnant. Once the words were out, the entire day's story came spilling forth. Unhesitatingly, he reached out and enfolded me in his arms. I broke down and wept, and he just held me. I was never more in love with my husband than in that moment and I wept even harder. It felt like a great burden had been lifted from my shoulders. I wouldn't have to figure this out alone, and in that moment things didn't seem too bad. No, we had not planned for this child, but he or she was on the way and we had the next nine months to get used to the idea and to figure out things. For the first time that day, I felt a tiny flicker of excitement ignite deep within me... we're gonna have a baby... I 'm going to have a baby. I'm going to have a baby!

I am grateful that I have never been faced with the rejection that some women get with a pregnancy, planned or otherwise. I have heard of women whose husbands have asked for a divorce when they found out that there was an unexpected or in Jamaican parlance 'buck up' pregnancy. I have heard stories of husbands whose children are grown and out of the house and whose wives have had a 'late' pregnancy, who pressure their wives with threats of divorce if they don't abort the baby. Then there are married women raising their child/children alone because their spouses refuse to share the responsibility of parenting. And some men deny having fathered a child, or disappear once the woman says she is pregnant. I can only imagine the great difficulties these women endure to go through a pregnancy and raise the child by themselves. I often see the young school girls going to the Women's Centre in their pregnant state or with their young babies. While I am thankful for the strong role the Women's Centre plays in helping these teenage mothers access a second chance to complete their high school education, my heart breaks as I think about what lies ahead of them... a child having a child. As I thought about all the varying circumstances, I realized that my own circumstance wasn't as bad as I had been feeling. There is a thought that I read on a blog which inspired me and it says:

"...happiness is not the absence of problems, but the ability to deal with them. Imagine all the wondrous things your mind might embrace if it weren't wrapped so tightly around your struggles."

The Word of God encourages us to "give thanks in all circumstances; for this is God's will for you in Christ Jesus"[1]. This is a verse of Scripture I knew quite well, and it entered into my situation in a new way that day, as I came into the understanding that while this child might not have been planned by Robert and me, his conception was no accident, for I believe that there are no accidents with God. My - our child's conception was an act of God. He was designed on purpose with a mission to be fulfilled in the world. I did not yet know how prophetic that thought was, and would not know for some time to come. This child is a gift... I thought about the babies in the Bible who came with a special mission – Moses, Samson, King David, baby Jesus, I felt encouraged, and my baby is in good company. Before I drifted off to sleep that night, I felt a surge of happiness... we're having a baby!

Chapter 3

Yes! We're Having a Baby

My mother was the first to know. She was very happy for us. As far as she was concerned it didn't matter if we had a dozen children, we were married, and the more grandchildren we gave her, the merrier! My sister Jennifer was next and she too was happy for us. One by one we called our immediate family members and told them about the pregnancy. The calls went better than I expected. The only person who threw a damper on this news was my father whose response was, "You having another baby again. Den you nuh just have one the other day?" "You mean Jordanne?" I replied, "She is three years old!"

We waited a while to tell our children. They were young and as they had not yet grasped the concept of time we knew they would expect to see the baby shortly after they were told of its pending arrival. We broke the news to them at six weeks and they were elated. After that, every hour on the hour one of them would ask, "Mommy, when is the baby coming?" I would say not for a while and the next question would be, "What is taking it so long?" To keep my sanity and to help address these important concerns, I purchased a children's book on pregnancy. There were beautiful 3D images that showed the baby's development at the different stages. They were elated. They studied this book intently every day – before school, after school, and two to three times a day on the weekends! They engaged each other in deep discussions about what was going on with the baby at each stage. It was precious to see how absorbed they were in the pregnancy. They declared to all visitors that, "We're having a baby!" And would pull out the book to give the listeners, their 'expert' explanation of our baby's development. With each passing week, the excitement of the pregnancy and the expectancy for our new baby blossomed. We were all excited. The earlier trepidations now a distant memory.

From the very first day, this pregnancy had been fierce and I felt like I was being beaten up from the inside out. I had very bad morning sickness which I never had with my other children and my stomach seemed to be on fire all of the time. To help take my mind off my discomfort we launched a little 'naming our baby competition' – boys against girls. The girls wanted another little girl, but Ryan was a fierce defender of 'boy power' and felt that we already had an imbalance with the girls outnumbering the boys three to two including Robert and me. So in his 'expert' opinion it was only fair that we should have a boy. Remembering the evening I sat in the car before telling Robert about the baby, I too secretly believed we were having a boy. I know the differences between the sexes in pregnancy, having found the girls were easy to carry while the boy was very hard on my body.

For some reason, we settle on only two male names – Jonathan and Nathan. Both meant 'God's Gift' or 'Gift from God'. Robert and Ryan preferred Nathan while the girls and I preferred Jonathan. So we wrote the two names down and waited to see whose would win. When I was four months pregnant, two things happened. Adrianne, our eldest, told me that she and Jordanne had decided that it no longer mattered whether we were having a boy or a girl. All that mattered was that we were going to have a baby and so they would take whichever came. Shortly after that, Robert told me that he preferred the name Nathan because biblically, while Jonathan was King Saul's son and a faithful and

Raising Nathan

loyal friend to David, Nathan was a God-honouring prophet who chastised David when he committed a sin with Bathsheba[1]. He felt that this was significant and that Nathan would be a more fitting name for our son. I had also read that those named Nathan tend to be a powerful force on those whose lives they touch, and that they are capable, charismatic leaders who live the name, who often undertake large endeavors with great success. These were deciding factors... Nathan was definitely the name for our baby, so we settled on **Nathan** – even though we did not know yet whether we were having a boy or a girl! We were now down to only one name.

Chapter 4
It All Came Tumbling Down

Mrs Ebanks!" I was jolted back to reality. I was sitting in Dr Sideman's office. Everything came flooding back. I was waiting for him to tell us why the ultrasound check had disturbed him. I focused my mind on the present. It was time that I found out what was going on. We had come too far and were going through too much to be defeated at this juncture. I was ready and so I mentally braced myself to take on whatever we needed to face.

Dr Sideman pushed the printout from the ultrasound scan towards us. I looked at the paper, but all I saw was a hotchpotch of blotchy white, grey and dark spots. I looked up at Dr Sideman and said, "I don't understand, what are you showing me?" With a pencil he began tracing an outline on the image as he continued. "As I was completing the scan I noticed something that I had not seen before." He then traced a thin, almost invisible white line. It was fine, but I was soon to discover its significance. Dr Sideman continued, "I noticed that there is fluid in areas where fluid should not be. This is the outline of your baby. This is his chest; here is his right lung which is fine, but over here where his left lung should be I am seeing a pocket of fluid. This is what those white spots are. And if there is fluid in this area, then it means that the development of this lung is incomplete."

He continued to trace the image and to describe all the little abnormal slips of white that I could now see, now that I knew what I was looking for. He sat back in his chair seeming to organize his thoughts as if searching for a way to continue his explanation. "Your baby is very ill. He has a condition called a congenital dia- phragmatic hernia." "What?" I asked. I was confused and asked him to explain. He paused as if to gather his thoughts again before continuing, "I have only read about his condition and have never before encoun- tered it in my years of practice. It is a rare condition which is reported to affect mainly boys, and what it means is that your son has a hole in his diaphragm which has caused all of his intestines to fall into his chest cavity and compressed his left lung and pushed his heart over to the right side." I was speechless. So dumbfounded was I and immersed in what I was being

told that I missed hearing that we were having a boy.
It didn't matter. What now mattered and became
my number one priority was whether our baby
would survive!

Subsequently I did my own research to understand
clearly what the condition was all about. As I understand
it, the thoracic diaphragm is a sheet of internal skeletal
muscle that extends across the bottom of the rib cage.
The diaphragm separates the thoracic cavity (the
chest) containing the heart and lungs from the abdominal cavity (the stomach) which contains the small and
large intestines, and performs an important function
in respiration. A hernia is where parts of the lower
oesophagus or stomach that are normally in the abdomen bulge abnormally through the diaphragm and are
therefore present in the thorax (chest cavity). In a
foetus these hernias may occur as a result of malfor-
mation, hence a congenital diaphragmatic hernia.
When the affected membranes fail to fuse, the diaphragm
does not act as an effective barrier between the abdomen and thorax. Because the foetus is upside down
the contents of the abdomen, including the intestines,
press their way into the thorax and generally impact
on the development of the growing lungs. This leads to

hypoplasia, which is underdevelopment or incomplete development of a tissue or organ (in our baby's case his left lung).[1] Some of the startling facts I learned was that 1 in 2500 babies are diagnosed with Congenital Diaphragmatic Hernia (CDH) every year. The World Census Bureau estimates that in 2008 over 350,000 annually or 147 babies are born in the world every day with CDH. Now here is the startling part, this condition mostly affects boys! The research also indicates that the cause of CDH is still unknown, but this condition has been associated with several genetic anomalies such as Fryns Syndrome, Cornelia deLange System or Trisomy 18, 21, & 22.[2] I learned that the mortality rate in developed countries, where the technology is much more advanced, was a 50 percent chance of survival.

I heard the words, but my brain refused to process what I was hearing. So I asked Dr Sideman if this meant my baby was going to die. He replied that the baby was very ill and that I was now a high risk patient in need of careful monitoring so my baby could grow as large as possible, because he would require major corrective surgery at birth. He continued to speak but I was too deeply traumatized to hear anything else he had to say. He said something about picking up a letter to take to the University Hospital of the West Indies (UHWI) to transfer there so that my baby would have access to the Neonatal Intensive Care Unit (NICU) immediately after birth. I was currently registered with a private hospital and UHWI was semi-public and their policy was to register mothers within the first eight weeks of pregnancy. Though he didn't say it, I could tell that Dr Sideman was worried that I might not be accepted. After all I was now four months pregnant and with a bulbous tummy to show it. Nonetheless he asked that I return for a referral letter to take to the hospital's new patient clinic intake day as soon as possible.

I left the doctor's office that day forever changed. It was as if all of the colour had gone out of my world and was replaced with dark brooding storm clouds of fear, confusion, worry and deep uncertainty as to what the future had in store for us. It was hard to believe that in such a short space of time my outlook and circumstances could change so drastically. I became aware of Robert's presence as we walked to the car in a stupor. Not once did I consider what he might have been going through. I felt all alone and that this was my battle to bear. It is amazing to see how life plays out.

Raising Nathan

The night when Robert held me in his arms after learning that we were expecting, I had felt like we could take on anything together. Now in this time of need, I withdrew and opted to face my shock, pain and emotions alone...

We began the drive home in silence, both of us deep in our own thoughts. The meetings and pressing appointments we each had at work were the farthest things from our minds. My head was racing to make sense of what I had just heard. Maybe this wasn't quite as bad as it seemed. I grappled for answers. A scripture verse came flooding back and I recited it in my heart, "For you created my inmost being; you knit me together in my mother's womb. I praise you because I am fearfully and wonderfully made."[3] I couldn't quite remember where in the Bible it was from, but I latched on to it for comfort. As I mulled the doctor's words over and over in my mind, it came to me that we should talk to someone... but who? Our Church's nurture group leaders, Dave and Cathy came to mind.

Dave and Cathy Radlien were elders in our Church and our core leaders. Cores were nurture groups established by our Church to place each member into a small community group for fellowship and support. I was so glad that we could call upon older and more experienced parents (their children were mostly grown) and Christians who could provide us words of wisdom, encouragement and who would pray with us. Their home was beautifully appointed with a picturesque view of Stony Hill mount slopes and valleys and was located only a couple of blocks away from our apartment. I broke the silence to bounce this idea off Robert and he agreed. So I called Dave immediately. He answered on the first ring and I briefly explained what we had just learned, he listened intently and I could feel his support over the phone. Before I could make my request, he said, "Cathy and I would love to get together with you and Robert, can you come up to the house tonight at about six pm?" I was very relieved and confirmed that we would be there, before ending the call. I then called my mom in Florida and shared the news with her. I could sense that she was emotional about it, but she kept her calm and prayed with us. By the time I had finished making my calls we were at home and although the silence resumed, it wasn't the same as it was before the calls. The mood had lifted somewhat, because now we both felt supported.

Raising Nathan

Chapter 5

A Turn in the Tide

We arrived at the Radleins at six sharp and Dave and Cathy rushed out to meet us. Cathy gave me a big hug, while Dave led Robert off. She and I went to the living room and she began relating the experience from when one of their daughters had received abnormal test results when she was young. She shared their anguish and how through faith and prayer the Lord guided them to a medical facility in Canada that was able to help. By then Dave and Robert had joined us. Cathy shared how their faith in God grew as a result of the experience and how their daughter eventually received total healing. She anointed my tummy with consecrated olive oil as they prayed for us. We stayed only for a short while – it had been an emotional roller-coaster of a day and I was exhausted. However as we left for home, I felt like my child's odds for survival had just gone up some notches.

Raising Nathan

We eventually broke the news to our other family members, but like us, no one had a clue as to what the condition meant. However, over the next few weeks, the prognosis felt more and more unreal, and I settled back into just being pregnant, and living in hope that this was all a big mistake.

With Christmas now just around the corner, the ensuing weeks were very busy with holiday activities which helped to take my mind off of things. We had a great Christmas, but when January rolled in my mind was refocused on what was now needed... to register with the maternity unit of the University Hospital of the West Indies. It was going to be a long shot for me to be accepted but for some reason I was never worried or concerned. What was to be would be. I arrived at the hospital bright and early on the appointed in-take morning. I looked around the waiting room and none of the women present were visibly pregnant. They all stared at me, looking from my tummy to my face. I stuck out like a sore thumb, my tummy extended well before me. Registration was tediously slow but finally it was my turn with the intake nurse. She called my name and I rose and went to the desk. I handed her the referral letter from Dr Sideman and as she reached

for it, she looked up and saw my distended tummy.
I saw the shock register in her eyes. She looked up
at my face, then my tummy and back at my face.
Without a word she took the envelope I was holding,
opened it and read its contents. When she had finished
she looked up at me again, then back at my tummy,
and then asked me to take a seat. She regained her
composure and the registration process went smoothly.
The plan was that whilst I would have the baby at the
hospital, I would continue to be seen by Dr Sideman as
his private patient. This suited me fine.

My transition to UHWI was seamless. I saw Dr Sideman
there for my next visit and as Robert and I were leaving
the hospital following the visit, one of the nurses asked
if we knew where to find the maternity ward. Replying
that we did not, she gave us the directions and suggested
that we check it out before leaving. She explained that
had I been registered earlier I would have participated
in the antenatal classes and been taken through the
hospital on a familiarization tour. We took her advice
finding the ward easily, and then taking our own personal
tour asking a security guard and a nurse for information.
We were shown a side stairwell and told that was
where we should go to get to the delivery ward when

it was time for labour. I was told that if I needed assistance a porter would meet me at the car with a wheelchair to take me to the delivery room via an elevator. Satisfied, we left the hospital and returned home for the rest of the day.

Chapter 6

A Series of False Starts

About twelve midnight that same night, I awoke with sharp pains in my tummy. I was disoriented for a moment until the second wave of contractions hit me with a strong force. I was in labour... prematurely... I was only five months pregnant. I awakened Robert and within minutes he had his parents on the phone, asking them to come and pick up our little ones who were fast asleep. After a short wait, his dad arrived and we were on our way to the hospital.

We arrived just after one o'clock in the morning and I climbed the stairs to the labour ward. Despite the pains I was experiencing, I couldn't help but wonder whose idea it was to have a pregnant woman in labour climb a flight of stairs to get to the labour ward! We got to the receiving area incident free and I was processed and set up in a bed. My doctor came early in the morning and told me that I was experiencing premature labour and so they would give me some medications to stop the process and would keep me for a couple of days for further observations and to ensure that I settled before releasing me.

The next few days were torture. I ran my office from my bed much to the annoyance of the nurses who told me that the electrical outlet next to my bed was for medical use and not to charge my mobile phone. On occasions, they even threatened to take away my phone as I "Should be resting!" Four days, one dose of steroids (three shots) to help my baby's lungs develop, and eight bags of fluids (yes, I counted them because I hate needles and hate IV's even more) later, I was discharged with a stern warning to take it easy.

One month later, after mounting a major corporate event in Montego Bay for my company, I woke up around the same dead of night time of 12 o'clock with intense cramps. I was now seven months pregnant, and in premature labour again. This time, my doctor gave me cervical cerclage – the placement of stitches in the cervix to hold it closed. In my case, this procedure was used to keep my cervix, which was weak (otherwise called an incompetent cervix), from opening early, in order to prevent the progression of my

premature labour and early delivery. The aim of
my doctor was to keep my baby in for as close to the
forty weeks term as possible to increase his chances
of surviving the impending surgery that he needed.
This time I spent twelve days in hospital, receiving a
second dose of steroid injections (three shots) and 12
bags of fluids. I was released on condition that I go on
bed rest for the remainder of the pregnancy.

The weeks following my release were difficult. I had
never learned how to stay still and so I was in and out
of the hospital. My eight months hospitalization was
the worst of these visits. My doctor was away and so I
had the unfortunate experience of being seen by one
of the resident doctors. I awakened in the early morning with the telltale signs of labour and by now Robert
and I had it down to pat. We arrived at the hospital
and Robert went back home to get the children ready
for school. About 10:00am a youngish male doctor
whisked into my cubicle. His bedside manners were
dreadful. He marched in, picked up a chart and without
as much as a word proceeded to give me a very uncomfortable internal examination. Before I knew it, he
grabbed an instrument and began to cut out the stitches
that were in place. I told him I was not due for another

six weeks, and he finished up and picked up the chart he had earlier. He then asked if I was Ms so and so and I told him no. He said 'oops' and left. I never saw him again. When my doctor learned of this he was most upset. I then purposed in my heart that the next time I would return would be for the actual birth of my child. So I tried to stay in bed after that.

Chapter 7
Happy Birthday Baby?

The 36-week mark finally arrived though I felt like I had been pregnant forever. My doctor told me that while 40-weeks was ideal, it was safe for the baby to be delivered any day now. With this announcement the diagnosis which had sunk into the background became very real. It had been weeks since I felt any twinges of pain – I was ready for him to be born and so I began to venture out each day, moving around more and more trying to induce him to come. But he dug his heels in and remained put! I grew impatient and exceedingly tired. Finally my prayers were answered, four days into the 37th week I went to bed and at exactly midnight my waters broke with the gushing force of a powerful waterfall!

I was elated because I honestly felt like I did not have one more day left in me. The whole process had now taken its effect on me physically – my 5'4½" frame had ballooned up to 210lbs and I felt like my internal organs were being crushed. Mentally, I was also exhausted.

Raising Nathan

Robert sprang into action, D-day was finally here! He called Dr Sideman who told us to head directly to the hospital, and that he would meet us there. In less than half an hour we had arranged for our neighbour to stay with the children until Robert's parents could come and pick them up, and we were winging our way to the hospital. Because of the hour, the streets were clear and so a journey that could have taken 45 minutes to an hour, took less than 20 minutes.

By now I was well seasoned in getting settled on a labour ward and when we arrived there were nurses on the shift who knew me and knew my history. I was processed quickly. My labour was progressing swiftly with a strong force. I have often recounted to others, that while my pregnancies have been fairly good my deliveries have always been very hard, yet some-how after each of those deliveries it was as if a veil descended and the pain and trauma of the delivery vanished from my memory. I was not to be so lucky this time.

I arrived at the hospital around 12:50am and by the time I was settled and prepped it was about 1:30am, and I had already shed most of my amniotic fluid.

Happy Birthday Baby?

As the quality and intensity of the labour changed it was as if a floodgate had opened and the memory of the pain in all of my other deliveries came flooding in. I screamed in deep agony, pains so excruciating that I felt like I was losing my mind. I was overwhelmed and felt that I couldn't make it. I clutched at the hand of the nurse who was attending to me and screamed, "Nurse, I can't go through this again, I'm going to die!" The nurse pulled her hand away, smiled and said, "Mother, it is too late for those thoughts. Save your strength for the delivery." In desperation, I grabbed her hand again and said, "Nurse I want an epidural." The nurse laughed before telling me that it wasn't possible as it would have had to be arranged before as part of my birthing plan. Also it was just past 2am and there was no anaesthetist available, and by the time one would have gotten there I would have had my baby. Not to be deterred I blurted out, "Well I need something, give me drugs, strong drugs, any drugs!" She laughed indulgently and left the room.

This was one of the few times in my life that I felt mortally afraid. I turned on my side and prayed, "Dear God I can't do this again. I do not have the strength, please help me." Immediately I felt a gentle touch on my shoulder and a mature nurse I had not met before asked me if everything was all right. She had a kind face. I told her no, that I didn't think I could go through with a natural delivery. She said her shift had just ended but if I liked she could stay with me awhile. I liked that very much. Though Robert was in the room with me I felt a wave of comfort knowing that the nurse was there too.

The nurse sat beside me and then she did the strangest thing. Without a word she placed her hand on my stomach and prayed softly for me. I don't know what she said, but when she was done I felt a little better. The panic I was feeling moments before subsided. The pains remained though and she kept her hand on my stomach to feel the contractions. After a short while she had picked up the rhythm. Just before the next contraction hit she said softly, "A contraction is coming, take a deep breath and exhale slowly at the top of the contractions." I was desperate by now and willing to try anything and so I did as she said, but the pain knocked the breath out of me. With her hand still on my stomach she waited and again felt the rhythm of the oncoming contraction and repeated the instruction. I tried again and this time found that while the pain was still intense, the breathing exercise took the edge off the pain. We continued like that for 20 minutes or so. She talked to me quietly between contractions and I attempted to answer, but as the labour progressed it became increasingly difficult to concentrate or carry on a conversation.

When I had arrived at the hospital earlier that morning, the nurse on duty had said that I was just about two centimetres dilated. The nurse who now sat with me had checked shortly before departing at about 3:00am, and said that I was approximately three centimeters dilated. About half an hour later the contraction pattern and intensity changed once again – I knew the signs, I was nearing delivery. I tried breathing like the nurse had taught me but it no longer helped. I felt the baby drop down into the birthing canal, and no nurse was with me. I screamed for a nurse and Robert went to find one, but none came. I felt the familiar feelings that signaled that I had moved into the final stages of labour and the baby was getting ready to come. I screamed for the nurse again and when no one responded I screamed yet again, this time even more loudly, "Nurse, the baby is coming!"

Raising Nathan

A short older lady, who I later learned was the matron on duty, burst into the room briskly. "Why you making so much noise?" she asked. "You not ready to deliver as yet, we check you half an hour ago and you only three centimetres dilated. You have to dilate to ten centimetres before the baby can come!" I told her that this was my fourth pregnancy and I had a tendency to deliver swiftly due to having an incompetent cervix. That got her attention and she hurried over to check my cervix though she was still muttering that, "This was foolishness." As she was doing the examination I felt her body stiffen and she called for the porter to come and take me into the delivery room – I was now about eight centimetres dilated.

The matron got me settled on the bed before leaving again. I was alone. Robert was being prepped to come into the room. I was in the room by myself for what felt like about ten minutes when I felt the baby beginning to crown. My doctor had still not arrived and the matron was nowhere to be seen. None of the preparations in my birth plan were being observed. My plan instructed that because of the existing situation with the baby, because his left lung was not properly developed and there was fluid in that general area, the instruction

was that as soon as he was born and **_before_** the umbilical cord was cut, he was to be placed in an incubator.
But in that moment when my child started to enter
the world, I was alone in the labour room. The matron
was outside somewhere and Robert was still being
prepped. My doctor had not arrived and could not be
reached. There was no incubator... no pediatric team.

As the final waves of labour smashed into my body
I screamed. Something in the sound of that scream
must have communicated an urgency to Robert. He
later told me that when he heard that scream he knew
the time for our baby's appearance into the world had
come, but the attending nurses were unmoved. The
matron was beside him on the phone so he told her
someone needed to come to me now. Her response
was that there was no doctor and she didn't think
the baby was ready and that I was, "making a noise
unnecessarily." Without being fazed, my husband told
her that if anything were to happen to the baby he
would sue both her and the hospital. That got her
moving and she rushed into the delivery room. She
stormed in and was mad, but as soon as she saw my
position and realized that the baby's head was visible,
she panicked. She tried to squeeze my legs together

telling me to stop the baby's arrival until a doctor came! Not that I would ever have entertained her, but I had no control and within seconds my son entered the world. It was 4:25am on May 4th 2004.

Despite the unpreparedness and unprofessional conduct of the staff, my son's birth went well. Within minutes of his arrival the room bustled with people and a pediatric team of about four people took charge, setting our baby up on assisted breathing before they whisked him away. I did not even get to catch a glimpse of him. This was the first time that I was not given my baby right after birth. He was not even shown to me and it was later that I would come to realize the significance of that practice, and its role in effecting the bonding process of mother and child. Yes, during the pregnancy we had bonded. He was my little companion who went everywhere with me. But suddenly he had become a separate person from me and I never got the chance to even see him, to count his fingers and toes like I did his brother and sisters, to look into his eyes to say, "Hi there, happy birthday," like I did with my other babies, or even to simply touch him. This one seemingly simple omission would haunt me for many months to come, and would deeply impact our bonding in the early months and years ahead.

The nurse cleaned me up and I was moved to the recovery room. Not one word was shared with me about my child. Was he even alive? It was then that I realized that I had not heard the usual cry that had followed all of my previous deliveries. I felt naked, vulnerable and defeated in the hospital bed. It was as if I was forgotten. No one came to me. At 10am that morning I was checked over by one of the hospital's doctors, he was brisk and detached. I wasn't his patient and I felt it. My own doctor had still not arrived. As I waited to get some answers I thought the worst was over – but it had only just begun.

Raising Nathan

Chapter 8
50:50 Chance

The post-delivery ward was a large room with many beds. It was in full occupancy. Each bed had a curtain rail which allowed the nurses to close the curtains around that bed when they needed privacy. This was done during the scheduled check-ups, doctor's visit, when the patient was being washed or when there was an emergency. Outside of those times the curtains were pulled back and off to one corner of the space so that all patients were visible to the nursing station. Because the hospital is a teaching hospital, the newborns spent their time in a tiny bassinet beside their mother's bed, unlike at the private hospital where the babies are returned to the nursery at a set time. This I was told was to promote bonding between mother and baby and to facilitate the training of the mothers in all aspects of caring for a newborn. It didn't seem to matter whether it was the mother's first child or tenth, everyone went through the same process. At set times throughout the day, the nurses would have all the mothers put the babies on their breast, change them or cuddle them. It was like clockwork.

So I stood out like a sore thumb. I was the only mother on the ward whose bassinet was empty. This drove home the pain even more deeply. As I watched the other mothers kiss, coo, feed and snuggle their babies, I grew increasingly sad and depressed. My situation weighed down more and more heavily with each passing hour. I was wrapped up in worry, anxiety and self-pity. No one from the hospital team saw me or my pain. No one took the time to even look in my direction. It seemed like I was invisible.

The first time I knew that I was being watched, however, was when at one point I got up to go to the bathroom. I noticed that the women closest to me sprang into action and I saw with horror-filled eyes as each of them grabbed their baby from the bassinet and clutched them to their breast, staring at me with suspicious eyes until I was back in bed. I later learned that it is common practice for women who have lost their baby during the birthing process to steal another's baby. Having never delivered at a public hospital before this was news to me. I became very careful not to stare at the mothers and babies as I had before, just in case any of the mothers were thinking that I was devising a way to steal their baby.

It was now around 36 hours after my delivery. My doctor finally showed up. Without any explanation of why he was not there for the delivery, he proceeded to tell me that he had arranged for me to visit my son and the doctors there could take me through what was to follow. I was so glad that I would finally see my child that I opted not to talk to him about the medical neglect.

Robert arrived while the doctor was with me and we went together to meet with the paediatricians. I walked into the Neonatal Intensive Care Unit (NICU) and my heart fluttered to the floor when I saw all those tiny babies – frail and very sick – on the ward. With faltering steps I slowly followed the nurse. We came to a stop at a door leading to a small inner room within the ward. The nurse explained that this was where babies who were critically ill were put as the room housed the hospital's five neonatal incubators – though only four were in working order. We were lead into the room and I looked in shock at the four tiny bodies in the monstrous equipment... the equipment which was keeping them alive. Suddenly it dawned on me that I did not know which one was my son. I felt stupid. How could a mother not know the baby she had been carrying for the past 37½ weeks? Then I noticed that each incubator had a name tag and almost instantaneously I spotted my name. I walked up to the incubator and my legs buckled beneath me. I was not prepared for what I saw. My baby had tubes coming from all over his body – his throat, nose, chest, side and his private parts. He also had an IV needle going into him and his head was covered in surgical cloth. It covered his face like a mask, all the way down to the bridge of his nose. Here I was meeting my baby for the first time and I could not even see his face. I broke down and cried.

I was discharged that evening and went home with a heavy heart and a feeling of defeat. It was like I had run a race, won the gold medal but someone had forgotten to give me the prize. I was nervous beyond words because I did not know what to expect. No one had taken the time to speak with me – with us – to assist us to process what was happening or what was to come.

I did not sleep at all that night. The very next morning I crawled into our minivan at 7am and drove to the hospital to sit beside my son. This was to become my routine for the 24 days ahead. When I arrived I was in so much pain that I could barely walk from the car park to the building that housed the NICU. I could not even find a parking spot nearby and so had to park a great distance away from the building. By the time I got to the building I felt like I was going to pass out. Then I looked at the flights of stairs and again wondered who in their right mind designed the building to carry out its particular function. Don't they know the physical effects of child birth? It was sheer torture to get to the ward. But I persevered and after a while, I found I didn't mind the walk as it gave me time to be alone with my thoughts.

The team in the NICU were very nice. One of the unit doctors took a liking to our baby and this helped us to feel a little more comforted under the circumstances. We met with a number of different teams including the surgical team who explained that our baby was very sick, and what they were wanting to do. They wanted him to stabilize a bit more before they did the surgery to correct the breach and a date was set for

Raising Nathan

May 7th at 10am. The lead surgeon explained that the operation was a serious one which could lead to various complications, which she did not bother to get into with us. We were told that without the surgery our son would die and so naturally we signed the consent form.

For the days leading up to the surgery, I arrived at the hospital around at 8am to sit with my son. I sat by his side only leaving to go to the bathroom or to eat. I left the hospital at 5pm in the evening, praying and hoping that he would still be alive when I returned the following day. When I was at home in the evening, I was still on edge. Every time the phone rang I braced myself thinking that it was the hospital calling to inform us that our baby had died. To my great relief it was usually either a family member or friend calling to check up on us and to get an update on the baby. While the calls were very much appreciated, they were difficult and intrusive because I wanted to talk to no one. After a short while I stopped taking phone calls.

It was an exceedingly difficult time for all of us in my family. Robert had taken over complete care of our other children. And thankfully we had a housekeeper which helped somewhat. It was difficult having to travel to the hospital everyday, particularly so soon after giving birth. But it was more difficult to leave my tiny, defenceless child to fend for himself. He was kept on a fast for the first 11 days of his life and I was so heart-broken as I watched him cry, because though his mouth was open, there was no sound because of the tubes in his throat. He would cry for long periods of time in distress (and I believe from hunger). After a while he started to produce tears and this was even more heart-rending. As a result I didn't want him to be without one of us present, and while we could not be there round the clock, we were most of the time. I did the 8am to 5pm shift and Robert the 10pm to 12am shift. It was gruelling, but we would have it no other way. Our routine was simple, we woke up in the mornings, readied our other children and I would head out to the hospital while Robert took them to school. At 5pm each evening I would return home to care for our other children, while Robert went to school for his MBA studies. He would leave classes before they ended and go to the hospital which was next door to the university campus, where he would sit with our son until midnight. We kept a similar vigil on the weekends.

Raising Nathan

At no point did anyone offer to help us. This is not an indictment of anyone, but rather a recognition and acknowledgement that often when one is going through a traumatic experience, it is difficult for them to reach out and ask for help. I believe it is equally difficult for others looking on to know how to help or what to say. It is an uncomfortable situation all round.

As we continued this phase of our son's journey, we came to know some of the other parents. Robert shared with me that he had come to know a father whose baby was also in the NICU. The baby had been born prematurely at six months weighing two pounds. It was the gentleman's third child, each had come prematurely and the previous two had not survived more than a week. So he was deeply invested in this child and he sat with him from 6pm (after work) until 6am each day. He would freshen up in the Parents' Lounge before heading out to work. His son lived for three weeks before he passed away. Robert was there that night and said the father was devastated beyond words. This deepened my fear for our son and I believe that was part of the reason that spurred Robert to spend all of the time he could muster with our little boy.

A young resident doctor finishing her studies, Dr Sharon Smiles, took a shine to our baby and to us. She was assigned his case and I later learned from a nurse that she stopped in after Robert left each night and ran the 1am to 5am shift in between her rounds. She did so even during her preparation for her final examinations which she passed with flying colours.

Raising Nathan

Chapter 9

The Surgery

I arrived early on the morning of the surgery and watched as the team prepped my son. I was beside myself with worry. What if he doesn't make it? What if the surgeon makes a mistake? I had so many questions but could not voice them, and had no one to voice them to. The medical team did not see it as necessary to talk to me about the process. Robert had to go to work, but we lived on the phone that day.

I stood in the room as doctors and nurses bustled about, I was invisible. I stood away to a corner, watching, my heart was breaking as I was covering the proceedings, weeping silently for my son and praying for him. My heartline was connected to my child. Even though I had not seen his eyes open in all the days I was at the hospital, and it seemed that he was not aware of his surroundings, I felt that he knew I was there. I could tell in the way he reacted when I entered his room, or when I spoke I saw movement of his head towards the sound of my voice. It was ever so slight, and his brow would knit ever so softly, as if he was attempting to open his eyes. As I stood in the room that morning, I know that he knew that I was there, and in my heart I was holding him, hugging him, kissing his tiny face, although my heart felt like it was breaking in pieces.

After a while, the head surgeon turned to me as if recalling my presence for the first time and announced, "Mother, we will take your son to the theatre for surgery now." "How long will it take?" I asked. The surgeon looked at me briefly before responding, "I can't say." "This is major surgery," she continued, "And it depends on what we find when we go in." I guess I was seeking some reassurance, but her answer drove fear deeper into my heart. She then announced that I couldn't go with the team at this point but I was welcome to wait in the Parents' Lounge. I felt dismissed. I ignored her and as the team wheeled my son away I trailed after them at a safe distance. I just needed to know where they were taking him.

Because my son could not breathe by himself, a portable ventilator was used. I watched in quiet awe as the nurse pumped the breathing device with her hand. I felt panic rise in my heart. I thought back to the explanation given to me about why he needed a ventilator. Because his lungs were not fully developed he could not breathe on his own. Without help the carbon dioxide would back up in his body, and he would suffocate and die. My panic increased as I ran various scenarios through my mind's eye. What if the nurse's hand got tired and she stopped pumping? What if she tripped and fell as they were taking him to surgery? Did they even have a proper mechanical ventilator in the operating theatre?

I followed the team to the elevator and saw that it was set to go down. I ran down the brief flight of stairs and waited until the elevator arrived and the team alighted. I continued trailing after them, praying at the same time and hoping that my son felt my presence. I willed him to know that he was not alone and that I was with him in spirit. Finally the team stopped outside a door and a nurse from the inside opened it for them and the team entered. I hurried past and peeked inside just as the door was closing. I didn't have a clue as to what I was looking for but I just needed to see what was inside. I couldn't see much and so I took up guard a short distance from the door and waited.

Raising Nathan

Those were the longest hours of my life. As I waited my mind ran more scenarios, some of which didn't end too well. For the first time in my life I understood what it felt like to have someone battling for life. I tried to hold on to my faith but felt like I was losing the fight. My stomach was tied up in knots, and my body was assaulted by all kinds of emotions. After a while a porter came up to me and told me that I could not stay where I was. So I headed for the Parents' Lounge on the ward. I sat and watched the clock like my life depended on it. Every time the buzzer went off for someone to be let into the ward I jumped out of my seat and raced to the door to see if it was anyone with news.

Family members and friends who knew about the surgery kept calling and texting to ask for updates. This helped to create more anxiety for me, as while I knew they were worried I felt helpless when I couldn't tell them anything. One message was sent to me several times that day from a phone number I did not recognize – words that were also sent three days earlier, 'He will not die but live to proclaim the glory of God' (Psalm 118:17). I briefly mused as to what it meant and whether it was a Bible verse. But it wasn't long before I went back to my vigil – watch, worry, wait, pray.

My son was taken into the operating theatre at about 9am. It was now midday and there was no word from the team. I stalked the theatre several times and the same porter saw me each time. Finally I asked him whether anyone had come out of the theatre since that morning, and he said, "No." He then asked me to wait a minute and went up and knocked on the door.
A porter opened it from the inside and spoke with him briefly. He came back to say that the porter told him that the surgery had started late and so it was still under way. I returned to my position in the Parents' Lounge feeling a little relief – it meant that my son was still alive!

At about 2pm I saw the head of the NICU passing by the lounge. She hailed me when she saw me and I ran to her. I asked her if she had heard anything and she said, "No," but she asked me to wait a minute and went back to her office. I stood in the same place she left me and after a few minutes she returned to say she had called the theatre and the surgery was over for the most part, and they were cleaning him up.

Raising Nathan

I thanked her and breathed a sigh of relief. I returned to the lounge more relaxed than I was earlier but still wanting to hear how things went from the horse's mouth. About an hour later I saw the surgeon and made a beeline for her. She saw me coming but waited for me to ask her how the surgery went before she spoke. "Well," she responded. "You could say that the surgery was successful, if you want to call it that. I mean, there was very little blood loss and I guess that is good. We were able to push all of his intestines back into his bowels and repaired the breach." I felt elated, "Thank God," I started to say. "But," she continued as if I hadn't spoken, "It is too early to say if the surgery was a success." This alarmed me. "What do you mean?" I asked. "Well," she continued, "We had to use a new material to close the breach in his diaphragm and we can't say how his body will react. I mean his body might treat it as a pathogen and reject it." I felt the relief that I felt earlier dissipate rapidly. I stared at her in shock as she continued, "We also had to handle his intestines to push them back down into his stomach, we don't know what will happen to them so we have to wait and see." "What do you mean?" I asked again. She explained, "Well, when you touch internal organs the body has a way of rejecting the areas that were touched, so in this case while we tried to keep the handling to a minimum, we don't know how his body will react – we have seen instances where the areas handled wither up and die." I looked at her stunned and felt like I was withering and dying. This woman was killing me and didn't even seem to be aware of the impact of her words. She said some other things, but I had stopped listening, I had to hold on to the hope which I felt slipping away. I tuned her out and right there as she jabbered on I found her a new name, it was 'Dr Doom'.

In that moment I chose to believe that the operation went well and that my son would recover. I thanked the doctor politely and asked when I could see my child. She responded that he was in recovery and would be out in a couple of hours. I went back to the lounge and waited.

When he was finally returned to the ward and I was told I could see him, I was not prepared for the shock. He was more strung up with tubes than before. He had a large bandage wrapped around the middle of his body, he had tubes in his nose, throat, side and coming out of his diaper (nappy).

Raising Nathan

Thinking back I can't even fathom how I got through that day. When I saw him, he was awake and must have been in pain... he was crying. His mouth was open and he was making crying movements and tears were running down his tiny cheeks, but there was still no sound. I broke down and wept. He cried and I cried with him and the medical team working to set him back up in the incubator were seemingly oblivious to our pain. That night it was hard for me to leave him at the hospital. I was a nervous wreck. My head was pounding until I could barely see straight. I knew my blood pressure was dangerously elevated and that I needed to go home and get some rest. But how could I leave my baby after what he had been through that day? I called Robert at work and he decided that he would leave work early and skip his class to be with our son, and so I could leave. I felt a little better but still wanted to be there. I left the hospital at about 6pm that evening oblivious to the warning signs in my body that were telling me that I was not well. I went home but could not sleep. That was the night my insomnia began, and this would stay with me for the next three months, almost to the death of me.

The strain on our family over the ensuing days was tremendous. My blood pressure was dangerously elevated and could not be controlled with even the strongest medication. I had a headache every day and my whole body was riddled with pain. Robert was affected both physically and emotionally and I watched his shoulders sag as he went through the daily routine. We were both out of our mind with worry and grief. The financial strain brought on by the hospitalization was also great. Our children at home were equally affected. They were desperate to meet their new brother, and couldn't understand why he wasn't coming home.

Raising Nathan

Chapter 10

Fighting to Live: His Name is Nathan

The days immediately following the surgery were filled with worry as we waited, and I hoped and prayed that my baby would have a full and complete recovery. I sat by his bedside each day willing him to recover, willing him to open his eyes. I read the Bible to him, talked to him constantly and sang to him. I had started a tradition with each of my children of giving them what I call their own theme song. The song was a lullaby and I felt that each of them deserved to be treated as special, and the song I chose or made up represented their unique expression of themselves. The song I chose for my baby was the first verse and chorus of 'You'll Be in My Heart' by Phil Collins from Disney's 'Tarzan' soundtrack.

'You'll Be in My Heart' sung by Phil Collins

Come stop your crying
It will be alright
Just take my hand
Hold it tight

Raising Nathan

I will protect you
From all around you
I will be here
Don't you cry

For one so small,
You seem so strong
My arms will hold you,
Keep you safe and warm

This bond between us
Can't be broken
I will be here
Don't you cry

'Cause you'll be in my heart
Yes, you'll be in my heart
From this day on
Now and forever more

You'll be in my heart
No matter what they say
You'll be right here in my heart, always... always.

I developed a daily routine. Each day when I arrived at the hospital I would greet my baby with all the excitement I could muster in my voice. I would tell him all that happened at home the evening before and would give him butterfly kisses from his sisters, brothers, dad, grandparents and so on. I would read the Bible to him and then sing him his song. His eyes were closed as if he wasn't conscious, but as the days wore on I started to notice that his head slightly angled to the sound of my voice. I talked to him frequently throughout my time with him. I felt that he needed to know I was there, and since I didn't know what else to do I read, talked, sang and prayed.

He remained critical for days after the surgery and this worried me greatly. His situation was magnified by the fact that each day babies were dying all around him. It grew tougher each night when I had to leave him alone to go home – I felt like I was abandoning him, and my deepest fear was whether he would still be alive when I returned the next day. I noted the pattern that each night one of the babies in the NICU died, and by the time I arrived the next morning a new baby had taken his or her place.

Each day had its own trials and troubles. And I had a front row seat watching the dance for life, as babies fought for their lives. The four working incubators were always full, and it was heart-rending to return to the hospital the next day and see that one of the babies had gone. It was also common for one of the monitors to go crazy as a baby went into crisis, and to have a team rush in, usher us out of the room and try to save the child. Sometimes the team was successful, but too often they were not. It was hard to see the tell-tale green cloth covering the cot, where a short while before there was a life...

I left the hospital unwillingly each night. I wanted to stay with my son, it was as if a part of me believed that my being with him would make a difference. I hoped that he would live. While my heart prayed that he would, and I struggled to hold on to any vestige that indicated that he would live through this, on a deeper level my faith was being tested because I secretly knew that I was not fully convicted that he would live. With the constant fear of death and actually seeing babies die daily it was difficult not to get caught up in the drama of the hospital unit. Each evening as I reluctantly left for home all I could think about was that I would receive a phone call from the hospital in the night to say my son had passed away. The fear was so real that I would run the scenario in my head, and it went something like this.

The phone would ring and I would be in bed. Robert would answer the phone and I would know that it was the dreaded call. Robert would listen and say, "We'll be there," and then he would hang up the phone. With tears in his eyes he would turn to me and say, "Honey, that was the hospital, our son is gone." Always when it came to that point, I would physically shake myself and say, quoting from Psalm 118:17: "He will not die but live to declare the words of the Lord." These words from the mysterious text messages would chase the dark imaginings away for a while, but they always returned.

At the same time I missed my other children dearly and wanted to see them and spend time with them. I found that in those first few weeks of Nathan's birth, being around so much sadness and tragedy took me to a place of deep appreciation. Appreciation for what I had and have been given. I had gone through three pregnancies before and never knew that there was such a thing as a newborn baby being in crisis.

Raising Nathan

My nephew, who was born a few months after Ryan, was diagnosed with autism at about age two. I was pregnant at the time with Jordanne and so was caught up in my own world and had not paid as much attention as I should have. That was the closest I had come to a child with a challenge – besides flu, colds, allergies, a pumped stomach for eating pills out of the house-keeper's bag (Ryan was two and a half when it happened), an emergency visit to the hospital with burns to the hand, foot and just above the eye (Jordanne was 22 months and asleep when the housekeeper dropped a hot iron on her), and chicken pox, of course.

After departing the hospital each evening, during the 45 to 60 minute drive to get home, I would pray to the God of my Faith and plead with Him to keep my baby and watch over him for me until I returned the following day. I would go home physically – but spiritually, emotionally and mentally I stayed at the hospital. I was too distracted to do homework with my children so I would send them off to do their work alone.

I frankly don't know how we managed all those weeks. Trying to look after young children at home and be there for our new son. We barely spent time together

as a couple as we moved in opposite directions to keep
our family moving forward. By the time the children
went to bed at night I would collapse in bed, exhausted
and drained without measure, but sleep was always
elusive. Every time I tried to close my eyes I would
be jerked awake with the shrill ring of the telephone,
heart pounding, body suffused with sweat as I gingerly
lifted the phone, sure that this was the dreaded call.
Thankfully each time it was one of the well-intentioned
friends or family members calling to check in with
us. After the call ended I would lie awake waiting for
Robert to return home. I always breathed a word of
thanks when I heard his car pull into our driveway. I
would hear him tiptoe into our bedroom trying not to
waken me and though I was always happy that he was
home, I would lie still so he would think I was asleep.
Moments later I would hear his 'train station snoring',
as he would fall asleep right away from sheer exhaustion. I would then relax and stare into the darkness of
the bedroom and worry.

Each morning I couldn't wait to get going. There was
an excitement in my spirit, the kind that you feel when
you haven't seen a beloved one for a long time. I could
not wait to get to the hospital to see my son even

though his eyes remained closed and he gave no indication that he was aware of my presence. I would start the process all over again.

Trials are never without hopeful moments and Dr Smiles continued to be one of the bright spots in our valley of despair. Dr Smiles was true to her name – bubbly, beautiful, vivacious, warm, zesty, caring and inclusive. She was respectful to me as a mother and always knew the right thing to say. From the very first day I met her I took to her like bread to butter. She was easy to talk to, cared deeply and genuinely about her charge and was a strong Christian doctor. She was one of the few professionals on the ward who didn't talk down to me and who spent time explaining things and encouraged me to ask questions. Her presence helped me to keep my sanity throughout my son's time in NICU. We are forever grateful to her for this show of support and care and know that this went a long way into conveying to our baby that he was loved and cared for. I got the opportunity to tell her this when Nathan was four years old and we ran into her at Church.

Ten days after my son's birth and seven days after his surgery, I came to the hospital one morning and found the team in a mild panic. I walked into the unit and saw a group of nurses and doctors huddled together just inside the entrance. As I walked in one of them looked up and exclaimed, "Here she is now." For a moment I felt a wave of anxiety washed over me, but it dissipated just as quickly. "Here she is for what?" I asked nervously. The head of the Unit asked me to follow her to her office, closed the door behind us and took a seat. She then told me that they had been trying to reach me since earlier that morning, and that they had left a message at my home and on my mobile phone for me to get in touch with the unit as soon as possible. She thought I had come because I had received the message. She must have seen the panic rising on my face because she quickly launched into the reason they were trying to get in touch with me.

Around midnight the nurse on duty discovered that Nathan was running a high fever with all the signs of jaundice. They tested him and found that he had a high level of bilirubin. I did not understand the significance of what I had just been told. I knew a little about jaundice – the doctors had told me with each of my other children that they had newborn jaundice and that I was to put them in the early morning sun for ten to fifteen minutes daily for about ten days. The jaundice went away after a few days on its own. So when the doctor asked whether I knew what jaundice actually was, I shook my head 'no'. So she spelled it out for me. Jaundice is caused by a build-up of a substance called bilirubin in the blood and tissues of the body – hyperbilirubinemia. Bilirubin is made when the body breaks down old red blood cells. The liver helps to break down the bilirubin so it can be removed from the body through sweat, urine and stools. Any condition that disrupts the movement of bilirubin from the blood to the liver and out of the body can cause jaundice. In my son's case, though they were not entirely sure of the reason, it was highly suspected that this was as a result of the major trauma that he had undergone since birth as his organs were not yet functioning in the way they should.

I did not know what to say or how to respond to what I had just learned. So I remained silent so the doctor could continue and thankfully she did. She said ordinarily if the circumstances were different and my son was a healthy baby, they would not be as concerned as jaundice often appears within two to four days of birth in healthy babies, and usually clears up within one to two weeks. But in this case my baby was still very ill and so his body's normal healing and restorative mechanisms were not optimal.

"The problem is," she started and then she paused... "In your son's case his jaundice has appeared ten days after birth, seven days post surgery..." she paused again before continuing, "His bilirubin count is very high." "What do you mean?" I asked. "How high is it?" "408," she responded. Confused I asked, "What does that mean, what should the count be?" "Zero," she answered, "There should be no bilirubin in his blood, when there is, it is a sign that something has gone wrong." Now desperately searching for a small glimmer of hope I asked, "What level is considered dangerous?" "Anything over 100," she answered softly. I felt the breath knocked out of me and sat down heavily into the chair she had offered me when I first entered the office. "What is the course of action?" I asked. "That was why we were trying to reach you," she said. "We wanted to give your son a blood exchange transfusion,[1] but we needed your or your husband's consent. However, we encountered three problems, one was that we could not reach either of you, and the second was that we could not locate any whole blood that matched his blood type." "Thirdly," she added, "Because your son has not been responding well to treatment post-surgery we feel that he might not be able to survive the procedure."

Then for the first time she smiled. "Luckily we did not go that route because in wanting to start a treatment we went with phototherapy. We began treatment this morning at 6am and after two hours he is responding. The bilirubin level is dropping nicely." I cannot recall a time when I was so grateful to someone. I thanked her profusely before leaving quickly to go and see my baby. When I walked into the room and saw him however, I gasped in shock and for a moment felt the room spinning. I staggered backward and my back got caught up against the door. I steadied myself, braced myself and then pushing myself off the door walked purposefully to my son.

What had me reeling was that the IV drip that before had been in his hand or foot was now in his head. It was the most ghastly, barbaric and painful-looking thing I have ever seen. I quickly hailed a nurse and when she came over I asked what was going on. She explained that because of the number of drips my son had received so far the veins in his hands, arms and legs were swollen so they relocated the drip to his head. I found this very disturbing but under the circumstances had no choice but to allow it to be.

I focused myself on other things – after all, based on what the doctor had said about his jaundice, the bilirubin level was going down. I sat with him and began my daily routine of reading the Bible, singing and talking to him. I described our home, his brother, sisters, aunts, uncles, cousins and grandparents. I shared my dreams for him. I talked and talked. Finally at midday I was called to the doctor's office. She said that he was now out of danger, the result of the blood test they had taken two hours before was back and his bilirubin level was below 20 and still dropping. I could feel the tears prickling the back of my eyes as I exhaled with relief. I called Robert and shared the good news and then went back to sit with my baby and tell him the good news. I felt a turning point in his situation. What I didn't know was the irreversible damage that the spike in his bilirubin level had caused and the effect that it would leave behind. This would not come to light until eight months later.

Raising Nathan

On day 11, I could barely drag myself to the hospital.
By now the physical, mental and emotional exhaustion
had kicked in. Being hypertensive my blood pressure
was high... 160/120, and it wasn't dropping. I had a
continuous headache. I was exhausted and walking
any great distances left me gasping for breath. When I
arrived "Dr Doom" requested that i join her in the
consultation room. I went to see her and she launched
into a very sterile discussion about my son. She told
me that he was not responding to any treatment and
that he was just 'there'. She said that he might not
recover because he was still very sick. I could take
no more bad news so I turned off my ears. As I went
inside myself, I cried out silently to God and asked him
to do something. When she had finished speaking I
went outside to my minivan. As I was about to climb
into the vehicle I heard a voice saying to me, "Why are
you waiting for him to die?" I stopped in my tracks and
looked around, but there was no one near to me. So I
continued to open the car door. Right at that moment
the voice repeated with more volume and persistence,
"Why are you waiting for him to die?" Up until that
moment I had not faced the fact that I was sitting on
the fence concerning my baby's chance of survival.

I had bought into the 50:50 chance of survival that was presented to me.

I thought about the statement for a moment and then responded adamantly out loud, "I am not waiting for him to die, I want him to live." There were many emotions in that statement for I thought to myself, look at all that I have been doing, why would I want him to die?! The voice responded, "If you are not waiting for him to die, why isn't his bedroom at home ready for his arrival? Why have you not given him his name? What are you waiting for?" I thought about the questions for only a moment and then realized that the voice was right. I was sitting on the fence not vested either way. I was waiting to see the outcome. I was not exercising faith.

Standing in the same location, I called my pastor at Church – Pastor Merrick 'Al' Miller, a man on a mission and my spiritual father. I felt like I needed some spiritual backup. I could not reach Pastor Al as he is affectionately called by his flock, and when I briefed his secretary about the situation I found that the Church was not aware of what we had been going through. Understandably, Robert and I were too preoccupied, and having no close friends in the Church, there was no one to relay our situation. Outside of our son being born they did not know what we had been going through. I left a message that I – we – needed prayer and hung up. I then set out deliberately across the compound to get to the Records Office. When I located the office it was nearly empty, save for the lone person working. I gave her my name and delivery date and she was able to locate my records quickly because an officer had visited me the day my son was born and taken some of my details. I provided all the answers to the various questions, and when I was asked for my baby's given name, I spoke his name out loud for the first time since his birth, "His name is Nathan Kingsley Ebanks."

Kingsley is my husband's middle name, inherited from his father. Ryan, our first born boy, also has Kingsley as his middle name. At first saying his name – Nathan Kingsley Ebanks sounded strange. But as I walked back to the NICU, I kept repeating it out loud. I found the more I said it the more it became real and the easier it rolled off my tongue. Just as I got to the floor beneath the ward a call came in on my mobile phone. It was Pastor Redwood, one of the senior pastors from my Church. I was so glad for the call. Before I knew it everything came spilling out. I gushed on for a good while, crying through parts. Pastor Redwood listened. He then confirmed what I had just found out, that the Church did not know that we were going through all that we were. He told me that Pastor Al, who I had originally phoned, was on duty-travel overseas and asked if I minded him praying with me instead. I told him no and he began praying. I don't recall what he prayed, but part way through his prayer he stopped to say that as he was praying he saw a vision in his mind of Jesus cradling Nathan in the palm of his hand and that it is well; Nathan would be well. I wept shamelessly. When he was finished I hung up and for the first time I didn't feel the anxiety to rush back to my son's bed-side. I dried my eyes, called home and asked my house-keeper to prepare my baby's room. She asked me if he had been discharged and I told her that he would be coming home soon and I needed her to put up his cur-tains, prepare his crib and get his room ready.

Raising Nathan

Chapter 11

I Met a Mom

I started walking back to the NICU but as I entered I felt compelled to head for the Parents' Lounge. I had never felt an urge to sit in there before as my days were spent by my son's bedside. I only got up when I needed to stretch my legs or visit the bathroom, and I usually took lunch with me and would eat it in my minivan. This day in particular, however, I felt the urge to go and sit in the room for a while. It turned out to be my most defining moment at the hospital.

I arrived in the lounge and immediately noted that there were three mothers there. They turned when I entered the room and nodded their heads before resuming their conversation. Unintentionally I learned that one mother, whom I will call Mother #1, had a baby with a hole in his heart. He was born at a rural hospital but was taken into Kingston for surgery. He was not quite four months old and had been in the hospital all of his young life. The doctors didn't feel he was strong enough as yet for surgery and so they were keeping him in and trying to get him fit enough for the operation. His mother seemed a young woman under 30 and she had three young children at home.

The second woman, Mother #2, was an older woman. She was somewhere in her mid to late 30s, and was telling the others that this was her third pregnancy and that her body seemed to abort the pregnancies by the time they got to five months. She lived somewhere in Gordon Town in St Andrew, and her two previous pregnancies had ended badly as her babies were born at three months and five months respectively. She said that the doctors at the hospital had told her that they could not guarantee her an incubator for when her babies were born, and she lost both of them within hours of their birth. She registered at the hospital for her third pregnancy and at four months went into premature labour. The doctors were able to keep her baby in place until five and a half months. She said that two weeks previously she woke up covered in blood, and when she was rushed to the emergency ward she was told by the doctor in charge that again the hospital could not guarantee her an incubator. She said she had broken down and asked if they thought it was fair that they had told her that two times before

and lost her two babies, that they could tell her that a
third time. Her persistence won out and her baby got
an incubator. It was next to my son's.

Her story was further complicated, however, because
she was admitted to the hospital following the delivery
because she had 'sugar' and high blood pressure and
they were both out of control. I remember thinking
to myself that I had not heard of anyone having sugar
since my grandmother died about 20 years before,
I thought that sugar was eradicated! It was not until
a few months later that I found out that 'sugar' was
actually a colloquialism for diabetes.

The third woman's, Mother #3, baby was born at three
months old, weighing a mere one and a half pounds.
I remember thinking to myself that I have cooked
chickens bigger than him! But what really struck me
right away was that all the babies who were being
represented in that room were boys.

Before long I was drawn into the conversation. I gave
the shortened version of my story – my son's story.
The mothers had all arrived at the hospital long before us

and they brought me up to date with the 'happenings' – who was nice, who wasn't and so on. Then one of the mothers mentioned that of the more than 20 babies who were on the ward there were some who had never received a visitor... one had never even seen its mother. I asked her what she meant and she explained that she had never seen anyone come to visit some of the babies, and she told me where the babies were located.

I noticed that each day when I passed these babies they would make sounds and try to get my attention but I was told by the matron that I was not allowed to talk to or visit any baby but my own so I had kept my head straight. My heart broke to think that these tiny babies were in a fight for their lives and they had no one to love, comfort or be with them. I did notice, however, that the nurses were more attentive to some of these children and spent a lot more time talking with them, dressing them and cuddling them. There was one baby, a beautiful little girl, she had the most gorgeous eyes but they were unblinking. I was told she was born at another hospital and suffered brain damage. She was brought to the NICU on her six month birthday. I learned that she was the first child for her parents and her mom had gone into post-partum depression and couldn't see her. The nurses dressed her beautifully in a pink dress and pink bows in her hair. She died a few weeks later. Her passing chipped away a piece of my heart.

After a while two of the ladies left, but Mother #1 remained. We were silent for a while each lost in her own thoughts, and then without warning she asked what I did for a living. I told her that I was a senior market planning and corporate event executive and the company for which I worked. She responded that she knew I was a 'big shot person' and that she saw me come in every morning and head straight to my son. She said I didn't look friendly and approachable so she was afraid to try to talk to me. I felt bad because until then I had not noticed her, nor anyone else for that matter. I was so caught up in my own story that I failed to notice that there were others with their own stories.

She told me more about her situation. She was an unemployed mother of four from a very rural parish in Jamaica. She talked of her struggles and how her pregnancy had drawn her to God. She said she was

converted by a Jehovah's Witness and that she had
been going to Church for almost a year but had not
accepted Christ, because she did not know how. We
talked for a while about Christ and salvation and I
shared my own conversion story. She hung on to my
every word and when I was finished, she asked me
if I could lead her to Christ.

I had never led anyone to Christ before and felt shy.
But she was so confident that I could not say no. I also
thought, "What if she left the hospital that day and
died, could I carry that on my conscience?" I whispered
a word of prayer softly before standing with her to
pray. I told her to say what I said and prayed a prayer
of confession of sins, acknowledging Christ as the Lord
and asking Him to come into her heart. She repeated
the prayer and then I prayed for her. It felt strange
but it felt right. It somehow felt like this was supposed
to be, that my son was there at that time to meet her.
Strange, but that was how I felt.

She overflowed with gratitude. She said that even
though the circumstances that brought us there were
sad what with our babies being sick, she was grateful
that we shared the same space as we would never

otherwise have met. She called me 'my girl'. She said to me, "My girl, meh sorry that we meet under them circumstance here, because we baby sick, but me glad we meet. Because me doan think seh me and you woudda ever did meet, normally. But because we two baby them deh 'ere, we get to meet and me thank you." We spoke for a while longer and then we went our ways each to check on our baby. While I was talking with her I felt a strong urge to offer her my Bible which I kept in my car, and some money from my purse... it was about $1,500. The Bible was special. It was the treasured item my mom gave me when I was moving out on my own. I kept it in my car and over the years had scribbled reminders, thoughts, special events and other memorable information in it. So I was not inclined to part with it... urge or no urge. The money I didn't mind giving, but not my Bible. Besides, the car park was too far away and I wasn't in the mood to make the trek to the car and back. I shook off the feeling, bade her goodbye and went back to sit with my son. I was feeling better, inspired, pumped up, hopeful. I left at the end of that day with the encounter still fresh on my mind. For the first time since Nathan's birth, I left the hospital that evening and my mind was not on him.

Raising Nathan

I arrived at my usual time the next day and popped my head into the Parents' Lounge but none of the mothers were there. I checked periodically throughout the day and for the next few days but did not encounter any of them. I felt myself becoming concerned for Mother #1, because when we spoke she said that she returned home every Thursday and came back on a Sunday and that she had been doing that without breaking for the four months her son was at the hospital. I began to dread that something bad might have happened to her.

The following week, as I was walking in a little later than usual I heard shouts of, "My girl!" I looked inside the Parents' Lounge and there was Mother #1 with a big smile on her face. I was happy to see her and we greeted each other warmly. I asked her 'how come' she was just getting back and she explained that the day we spoke she used the last of her money to go back home to Clarendon and that she could not afford the bus fare to return until now. Immediately I felt reconvicted, so I excused myself and went to my car. I picked up my Bible and emptied my purse. I returned to the lounge and told her what had crossed my mind when we first spoke – that I had felt I was to give her the Bible and some funds but that I didn't obey and now I was making up for it. I gave her the Bible and the money. She was grateful for the money but overjoyed for the Bible. She said that she loved to read and that ever since she got saved she had wanted a full Bible. She said that the Church she attended gave her a New Testament and that she had read it multiple times over and was longing for the full Bible and that this was God's answer to her. I was moved and at the same time deeply repentant. We spoke for a while and then said our goodbyes.

I walked away from the lounge that morning feeling like I had done what I was sent there to do. I never saw her again. Instinctively I knew that Nathan's time there was now drawing to a close. I started expecting him to get better.

My feelings manifested themselves the very next day. I arrived at the hospital and went straight to the NICU as usual. I made my way to my son's ventilator but stopped in panic when I saw that he was no longer there and there was a new baby in his stead. I turned to see one of the nurses hurrying to me and telling me not to panic because my baby was doing well. Apparently during the night he had taken a turn for the better and he had been moved to an incubator in the outside ward. This meant that he was finally on the mend and would be making his way home. I was overjoyed.

That same day I was able to hold Nathan for the first time and breastfeed him. It was a joyful day. As I took him into my arms he opened his eyes and looked at me, and it was as if he knew who I was. He still had some of the tubes on him including the IV. When he was taken out of the incubator he was given oxygen through his nose. I kissed his forehead for the first time... it felt strange. With my other children I was able to hold them right away. Before their umbilical cord was cut the doctor would place the baby in my arms so my baby and I were able to bond right away. I was denied that with Nathan. I saw him for the first time hours after he was born, and held him for the first time 18 days after his birth.

But I didn't care, my baby had survived and I was grateful to have him in my arms. So many other mothers did not get to have that moment. One of them was Mother #2, her baby (the one and a half pound one) died the week before. Both mother and father were devastated. I sat holding Nathan, grateful that he was

one of the lucky ones, but sad at the same time for all
the babies who didn't make it.

One of the nurses on duty had spent a lot of time with
Nathan since he was brought into the unit. She asked
me about his siblings and I told her that he had two
sisters and a brother. I believe she was moved with
compassion because a while later she came to ask
if I wanted his siblings to meet him. Of course I did!
She told me to bring them to the hospital that Sunday
evening during her shift at 5pm and she would arrange
for them to meet. I could not wait to go home and
tell them the good news, and they were excited
beyond belief.

That Sunday afternoon at 5pm on the dot, Robert
arrived with the children. They could barely contain
their excitement. I wondered how the nurse would
do it since they were not allowed into the NICU and
Nathan still needed oxygen support. But she knew
what she was doing. She hooked up an oxygen tank
and took Nathan out of the incubator and put the
tubes in his nose. Then she wheeled him tank and all
to the entrance of the ward and allowed his siblings
to step inside to meet him. My eyes misted up when

Raising Nathan

I saw the gentle way they were hugging and kissing him and telling him how much they loved him and couldn't wait for him to come home. Jordanne wanted to know why her baby brother did not have any hair! I could see that the nurse was touched as well. When it was time to go, they reluctantly but obediently left, telling Nathan that they would see him at home soon. Their faiths were so strong that I was encouraged. That evening they were sad and said that they, "Missed him already." I completely understood, because I too was ready for my baby to come home.

Chapter 12

Homecoming

Nathan progressed quickly as soon as he was moved into the ward. Five days later I arrived at the ward and again he wasn't where I had left him the evening before. The nurses had smiles on their faces when I popped my head in to look into the incubator and there was another baby there. Surprisingly this time I was not alarmed. I headed back to the nurse's station and as I got near one pointed to a small cot close to the entrance. I glanced over and there was Nathan. His wires and oxygen tubes were gone! He was breathing on his own! Of course my first reaction was to ask, "Should he be doing that?" The nurse smiled and said, "That means your son is getting better, you may be able to take him home very soon." I was ecstatic. In his new bed I could pick him up whenever I wanted, dress him, hug and kiss him. For the first time I felt like his mother. Nathan was 20 days old.

Raising Nathan

Another four days later as soon as I entered the ward I was told by a nurse in passing that my baby was on the discharge roster for that day. I stepped out of the room to call Robert and my mom to tell them the good news. Both were beside themselves and my mom broke out into shouts of, "Hallelujahs," and "Praise the Lord!" When I went back in Dr Smiles called me into the consultation room. She cautioned that while Nathan was on the discharge roster the final say was in the hands of his attending surgeon, the one I had nicknamed Dr Doom. I was not about to let go of hope and so I prayed silently that all would go well.

Dr Doom and her team arrived at about 11:30am and began the rounds. When she got to Nathan she began her examination, listening to his heart and doing the routine checks. While she was examining him I snapped a photograph of them together. She asked me what that was for and I told her it was for his picture album, and that she may find that one day a little boy would come up to her and say, "I know you, I have a picture of you in my album." Her response was, "Slow down, your son is still very sick, we don't even know if he will survive childhood." What a downer. For a brief moment I wished she could understand how her approach sucked the hope out of hopeful hearts. I wished I could shake her and tell her that in this place hope is all parents and families have, and that it was cruel of her to try to take that away. But I chose to remain positive and resolved in my heart that my son was coming home that day, home where he would be loved, supported and filled with positive energy.

After the checks, Dr Doom and Dr Smiles met with me in the consultation room. Dr Doom said that while Nathan was recovering nicely she was concerned that his wound from the surgery was not sufficiently healed for him to leave the hospital. I told her that if that was all, that I could and would do whatever he needed at home. I told her I have cleaned many cuts, scratches and accidents with his siblings so cleaning my baby's wound would not faze me!

She looked up at me when I said that and held my eyes for a moment before lowering her head again to the chart she was holding in her hands. Dr Smiles chipped in to say she had been observing me since Nathan was admitted into the unit and was impressed with my confidence in handling him and caring for him, and that she had no doubt that he would be better off at home for the rest of his recovery. Dr Doom wrote some more on the chart and then stated, "Baby Ebanks can go home today, I have signed his discharge sheet." I could not believe my ears. I felt the tears threatening to flow but held myself in check.

The discharge process went smoothly and Robert came to assist me in taking Nathan home. At about 2pm we left the hospital and took our baby home. It was May 28th, 24 days after he was born. I left the hospital that day thankful that my son and our family had survived this major ordeal and that the worst was behind us. Little did I know that it was the end of one chapter and only the beginning of the rest.

Chapter 13

Welcome Home Baby

Nathan received a warm welcome at home. My husband's parents and my sister Jennifer were the first to visit him, and a stream of friends and co-workers came. The ensuing days were tough as he adjusted to home and we adjusted to having a baby in the house. The gruelling schedule I had kept up during his time in the hospital had now finally caught up and I was feeling very sick and weak. Though it was difficult for me to move about and I had to rest frequently even during very simple activities, I faithfully changed Nathan's bandage and dressing as the nurse had shown me. Two days after he was discharged I got a home visit from a nurse from the hospital to see how we were getting along. She was impressed with how well I was keeping his dressing and asked whether I had medical training. I told her that necessity was the mother of invention and that I had three older children and so my skills had been honed! She smiled before leaving. Nathan was scheduled to return to the ward the following week, and again a week after that for checks. He was discharged to the post-surgery clinic – which is where things started to fall apart.

During the hospital discharge I had been asked whether I would be taking Nathan to the University Hospital's Paediatric Clinic for his well-baby checkups. I told the nurse no, that I would take him to the same paediatrician as my other children. At no point during the discharge consultation nor the four post-surgery clinics that I took Nathan to after, were we even alerted that because of what Nathan had been through, he was now at risk of developmental delays. At no point was I referred to or told that he would require early stimulation. I believe that this was gross negligence on the part of the hospital and it contributed significantly to what was to follow. I left the consultation that day under the illusion that all was well, and that my son would 'recover' given time.

The joy of bringing Nathan home was soon overshadowed by the reality of his care. He was still sick and medically fragile, and within days I knew I was out of my depth. He was still on breast milk exclusively and had a poor appetite. He was constantly spitting up or throwing up whatever he ate. I raised the concern at the very next post-surgery visit and was told that Nathan had a condition, gastroesophageal reflux disease, which happens when the milk a baby has swallowed comes back up into his food pipe (oesophagus), or into his mouth.[1]

The doctor from the University Hospital's outpatient clinic told me to come and get a prescription as my baby could choke on the reflux food and suffocate. The prescription was to be taken before meals for the rest of his life. I refused to believe that my child who was barely two months could be sentenced to such a fate, and so I prayed. I bought the medication, gave him the first dose and he spat it out almost as a projectile. This confirmed my gut feeling that he did not need the meds. So I decided to seek a second opinion from his primary paediatrician.

The paediatrician told me that the medication was dangerous as the side effects could turn out worse than the condition. She told me that I should hold off the treatment and try some natural remedies first. I was all for that.

They included:

- Feeding him in an upright position.

- Holding him upright for 20 minutes or 30 minutes after each feed. We found that it worked best when he was held upright for at least 60 minutes or more. This was particularly challenging as it meant almost holding him round the clock.

- Giving him smaller and more frequent feeds. This was the toughest one to adhere to as it meant holding him upright often throughout the night, which was exhausting.

Within days, we began to notice a reduction in the number of times he was throwing up and by the end of the month it was reduced to about 20 percent. But by the time we got the reflux under better control, we were hit with severe constipation. Nathan wouldn't pass his stool for days at a time and on one occasion went up to almost two weeks without having a bowel movement. This caused him to have severe abdominal pains and at times I had to stand up for hours holding him in warm water before he could get any relief. When he did go he experienced so much pain that it made him afraid to go, making his condition worse.

During one of his worst bouts when he was only about six months old, I stood with him in his bath of once warm water while he cried furiously. I was out of ideas, out of strength and feeling weak so I did the only thing I knew to do, I cried along with him. There we were, Robert was at work, the children were at school and the housekeeper was outside doing the laundry – and Nathan and I were in the bathroom crying together. Then something amazing happened. My baby looked into my eyes and through his tear-streaked face, flushed red from crying and straining to go, he smiled at me. It was as if he was reassuring me and saying, "Please mommy, don't cry." My heart melted because I should be the one comforting him, and though he was in pain he was comforting me.

Myths and misconceptions about disability are common. These incorrect assumptions are often triggered by fear, lack of understanding and/or prejudice. In that moment, as I was there with my son who was in pain caused by his constipation, I racked my brain to think of what to do. Suddenly, I remembered that I had once heard (not sure where I heard or might have read it) that these types of sickness can have a spiritual root, which in that moment I interpreted as having to do with some sin that I may have committed in the past. In desperation, even though I knew better, I fell back on the thought that maybe if I confessed my sin, then God may help my son. And so right there in the tub, I started to pray. I started confessing every sin and wrong doing I could remember, asking for God's forgiveness and intervention. I did this because I didn't know what else to do – I had given Nathan a pediatric enema earlier that day and it did not work. My actions were also out of fear, because the last time we had gone to the doctor with an issue of constipation, she had said that if the problem persisted it may mean that there was obstruction somewhere in his intestines – which was not uncommon given the nature of his surgery shortly after birth. She had said that she would recommend for Nathan to have a colostomy, which was, as she explained, a surgical procedure that brings one end of the large intestine out through an opening (stoma) made in the abdominal wall, to move the stool through his intestine through the stoma and into a bag which they would attach to the abdomen.

This would be a permanent situation! I was both horrified and determined that my son would never need such a procedure as it would never come to that. I had encountered only one person in my life that had such a procedure, and all I could remember was the unpleasant odour of waste that travelled with the person. I did not want that for my baby – he had already been through too much.

Suddenly in the midst of me praying and without warning I heard a loud plop and saw that Nathan had made the bowel movement into the water. I cannot recall that there was ever a time that I viewed such an act as a major accomplishment and celebrated! For every mother who has a child who has battled constipation, you know what I am talking about. The sheer relief and joy you feel that your child has gotten relief is indescribable. I bowed my head and prayed thanking God out loud, and at the end of my brief prayer I am sure that Nathan's bright smile was him saying, "Amen!"

I want to speak for a brief moment to the widespread myth of the 'sin of the parent or parents causing a child to have a disability' that had me caught up in the moment of this crisis. One of the most common myths is that the reason a child is born with a disability for example being blind, deaf or hard of hearing, or a physical or intellectual disability is because God is angry with the parents because they (the parent or parents) had sinned. This myth has been around a very long time, and there is even an account as far back as in the Bible in the book of St John in the New Testament, when Jesus' disciples having encountered a man who was said to have been born blind, asked Jesus the question, "Who had sinned, the man or his parents why he was born blind?" Jesus' response was, "Neither the man or his parents sinned..." The point I wish to make here is that many of these folklores are still alive and thriving today, and continue to feed the embarrassment, shame and negative stigma associated with having a disability. Because right there in that moment, when I was at my weakest, even I, an educated and informed parent, resorted to faulty thinking. While I did believe that God heard my prayers that day and helped Nathan, I do not for a moment believe that my son's condition was in any way, shape or form a punishment from God for my or my husband's sin.

Later that evening, after the crisis had began to fade,
I laid in bed reflecting on the many things that
we often take for granted, such as being able to
relieve ourselves unrestricted, my mind went back
to remembering a tragedy that occurred when the
bowels don't work the way they should. During
Nathan's stay in the NICU there was a newborn who
was brought on the ward with a maldevelopment in his
stomach – his intestines were wrapped up in knots on
the outside of his body. He was a beautiful baby boy,
born about one week after Nathan to a very young
mother. I realized that the mother may have been a
teenager because her mother was also allowed to come
into the ward when she came to visit her
son, and the rule was that only the birth parents
were allowed on the ward.

What made her stand out to me initially was that I
used to hear some of the other mothers jokingly call
her 'milk factory' because of the volumes of breast
milk she could produce while most of the others struggled to produce a few ounces each day. She would always
come in the morning with at least 12 three-ounce bottles of expressed milk, while the average mother could
barely fill one bottle. There were four babies in the

Raising Nathan

NICU including Nathan and the baby in question, when one of the monitors went off and a team rushed into the room and ushered us out. The screen was drawn right away to block out the view – this was usually a sign of an emergency, one of the babies was in crisis. Of all four babies, only I and one other mother were present and we prayed that it was neither of our babies who was in trouble. After a short while we heard one of the doctors asking where the mother was, and the nurse responding that she had not yet arrived but that she should come in soon. I breathed a sigh of relief as I realized that it wasn't Nathan. Nonetheless I prayed for all of the babies that they would be okay.

After a short while most of the personnel who had gone into the room left except for the nursing team. The curtains were still drawn and when the door was opened to let the staff out, I peeked into the room before the door closed and saw the tell-tale sign of the green hospital cloth covering the incubator where the baby was. The child had died.

As the door closed, as if on cue, the entrance door to the ward opened and the baby's mother and her mother came walking in. She was laden with bottles of breast milk and looking very relaxed. As I watched I could not believe my eyes and ears. One of the nurses saw her come in and walked up to her and said, "Yuh baby just dead eenuh. Im stomach burst open." Before she could say another word the mother fainted. From the bits and pieces I gathered afterwards, the baby had been given breast milk from the evening before, and because he could not have a bowel motion, his bowels ruptured. While my heart went out for the baby and mother this added another thing to my list of fear of what could go wrong with Nathan.

This memory helped to fuel my prayer that day and watered my thanksgiving that evening. Thankfully, that was not to be Nathan's fate. After that day I began to learn how to manage the constipation so as to never allow it to get to that chronic stage again. Nathan has had two other major constipation episodes over the years, including a hospitalization in a Florida hospital, while he was there undergoing intensive therapy intervention in 2007, but that is a story for another time. The lesson learned from this experience is that early identification, management and early intervention are keys to managing constipation. However, sometimes with even the best of efforts, he can still become backed up, when this happens applying safe elimination techniques – for example, using an approved pediatric enema, or gently massaging the child's abdomen works. In case these do not work, take the child to see a doctor immediately.

Thankfully a colostomy was not in my son's future.

Chapter 14
Early Warning Signs

Another myth that I would like to address is the one which states that children with developmental delays 'will grow out of their problems'. Paediatricians and child development specialists know that there is a very wide range in what is considered 'normal' or to use the more modern language 'typical' in how babies and children grow and develop. This varies from the very 'bright' children who seem to race through their developmental milestones, like my daughter Adrianne who was zooming so fast that she was up and cruising around the house by six and a half months. Then there are those who take a little longer time to learn new things or to develop. We also know that while babies and children all pass through more or less the same stages of development, they do so at different rates – each child develops at his or her own pace and the range of 'normal' is quite wide. This is important for parents to bear in mind and to accept that growing and learning is not a smooth path and that there are lots of ups and downs on the way. Child development specialists urge parents to apply as a good rule of thumb that comparing your baby or child with another, while it is interesting, may not be very useful in judging how your child is growing and developing. With that said, however, there are those times when there is definitely something more going on than meets the eye... As children develop, it is helpful for us as parents, and those who watch over their development, to be aware of common 'red flags' for potential developmental delays in children, so that we can act early. Early identification and intervention are the key to successful management of the situation.

In Nathan's case, because I was never prepared for anything to go wrong, I wasn't looking for signs; though they were right before me and glaring, I missed them for a while. But in retrospect I wasn't prepared for what I would have found anyway. I was an uninformed parent and didn't know it as yet.

The earliest warning sign which indicated that something was wrong with Nathan's development was seen at about two months. He had been at home for about a month and I was his primary caregiver. I had fallen ill from the entire ordeal. My dangerously heightened blood pressure, the prevailing insomnia, physical exhaustion and stress were now taking a toll on me. My doctor was concerned and at one point there was some talk about hospitalizing me if we could not bring my blood pressure under control. The doctor was very understanding however – as she had kept in contact with me during the pregnancy and so was fully cognizant of what I had been through. So she was lenient with me.

I was on a rigid routine of medicines but found that I felt sicklier and grew weaker each day. Despite all of this my primary concern was for Nathan, so while I did have help at home during the day, I wanted to care for him myself, and I did. Then one day I fell so sick that I was sure I was going to die. I could feel my body shutting down. I had difficulty breathing even if I only walked across my bedroom. That night as I lay in bed, I was afraid to close my eyes. I asked Robert to watch over me and to pray for me as I felt like I would not make it through the night. Robert was so beside himself with fright, that I was sure that even after the moment passed and I was alright, he had difficulty going to sleep.

Raising Nathan

As I lay in bed that night, I remember my Pastor teaching one day that every life which comes into the world was sent by God for a purpose, and that if that purpose was not yet completed we had the authority to tell death 'not yet' if it comes prematurely. That night I was certain that death was stalking at my bedside prematurely. For as I reasoned, God is a God of order and purpose. While He is Almighty, All Wise and All Knowing, I did not feel in my heart that He gave me Nathan and took him through what he had been through to take me home then. That night I reasoned with God. I prayed "Father, I thank you for taking my son through his ordeal. While I know you could use anyone else to raise him, you gave him to me. I feel that his purpose is wrapped up in my heart and intertwined with mine. So I am asking you to spare my life so that I may raise my son for you." Then I closed my eyes and slept. And for the first time in nearly three months, I slept in a deep REM uninterrupted sleep for 14 hours straight. I awoke the next day with the morning well spent and for the first time, I felt like my old self. I was on the mend. God had answered my prayer.

I was jubilant and overflowing with gratitude. As I opened my Bible which spent the night on the bed beside me, it opened on a scripture that I had never read before. The account was of Hezekiah in second Kings Chapter 20. Hezekiah was sick to the point of death. Realizing that the Lord favours those who earnestly serve Him Hezekiah appealed to God to favour him. The Scriptures tell us that the Lord responded by promising Hezekiah to add 'fifteen (more) years' to his life, and He did. I was wonderfully surprised. The scripture lined up with what I had believed the night before. Until that time, I did not know that an extension of one's life was possible.

As I began to mend, I noted sadly that my son did not. For instance, I found his interaction with me and with the world were still similar to that of a newborn. Each day his routine mainly comprised of eating at two to three hour intervals and sleeping. Overall he was lethargic and his body was floppy with no muscle tone. When I held him, it didn't feel like I was holding a person, it was like holding limp noodles. This was distressing for me as I found that if I wasn't careful and held him just right, he would slip through my hands or slide off of my lap. This made me very tense when I was with him, and added to the reasons I did not want anyone else but me handling him..

Raising Nathan

What this translated to in the early days of my relationship with my son was that I was caught up in the
role of a caregiver – including cleaning and dressing
his surgical wound which was a large incision that ran
asymmetrically from his left chest across and down
his right side covering one half of his body. It would
take another six months before it was fully healed
and another two years before Nathan was able to rest
on his tummy without fear. I also did his meal preparations, feeding, managing his medications, numerous
doctors' appointments, managing his many health
crises, bathing and dressing. I tried to do everything,
it was no wonder that I remained sick for most of the
three months post his birth. It was too much for me
to handle, but at that time it was something to do and
it made me feel useful. It also kept me tired so that I
wouldn't have to think about what was happening to
him. In all that was going on, there was a dark cloud
of tumultuous emotions which dogged at my steps. At
nights when the house had settled down and all was
quiet I would lie in bed, sleep was illusive and worry
would keep me company. It would be hours before
I would succumb to the blissful cloud of sleep that
would engulf me... only to hear the wail of the alarm
which would signal the start of another day. I would

crawl out of bed and begin the same nightmare all over again.

It would break my heart each day when I would see no positive difference in my son's development. I held him for hours at a time willing his body to respond to my touch. Praying that I would get some signal that he was aware of my presence, of our world. But the signs of engagement which one gets when one holds a baby, whether newborn or otherwise, were missing. Nathan's eyes remained closed most of the time, and when they were open there was no focus. He seemed oblivious to the world going on around him. Even though I felt something was wrong, I stifled the feeling, hoping that it was all in my mind. I was in denial. The paediatrician who saw him at the time didn't seem overly perturbed so I took my cue from him. If his doctor wasn't worried, why should I be? But it was easier said than done, because I would lie awake at night worrying and praying for my child.

Another thing that I wasn't proud of was how frail his body was – he didn't have the plumpness and lustre of a young baby. He ate poorly and would regurgitate much of what he ate so I was also concerned for his nutrition. I became very watchful over him, looking for all the things that were wrong with him and needed to be 'fixed'. There is an old saying that 'whatever you look for you will find', and that is certainly what happened in my case. The more I read about the development milestones of babies the more I saw the deficits in my child. This discouraged me greatly because I felt that my son was lacking in every respect and somehow it was entirely my fault.

As I looked I started noticing other things. The way his little hands were tightly fisted most of the time, the way his whole body writhed when he was eating as if he was a puppet on a string and his mouth was connected to every other part of his body. Or the way he would slide out of my arms and begin to fall if I wasn't holding him just right. I also noticed that he did not respond to any form of noise around him – even the kind made by his siblings, which I was pretty sure were loud enough to raise even the dead! This introduced another level of worry. Was he deaf?

My three months maternity leave was drawing to a close and soon I would have to go back to work, but I was unsettled. The growing suspicion that something was definitely wrong with Nathan started to flood my mind but I kept pushing it aside, hoping against hope that it was all in my head and that Nathan would catch up and get back on track.

In my early days as a mother I had come to learn from my mom that you begin to train baby girls to sit at two months by propping them up on a surface – a settee, chair or bath pan – with pillows to help to train them to sit upright and supported. I had done that with my girls and found it very effective. In fact, when I propped up my second daughter and third child Jordanne for the first time at two months she just sat erect and upright and looked around at us with a big smile on her face as if to say, "Look at me, aren't I great!"

I learned that boys are propped up a little later at three months. I had never asked why but had dutifully done so with my second born and first son Ryan. He took a little more time to get used to the idea of sitting up than his sisters, but he caught on soon enough and before he was four months old he had developed the skill of sitting. So I had no forewarning of what was to come with Nathan. On the three month marker I dutifully crafted a seat using pillows in a wash basin and put Nathan in it. I carefully made a ring of pillows and placed him in a sitting position in the centre. He promptly fell forward. I propped him up from every angle but each time I changed the position of the pillows he would fall in a different direction. After about two weeks of trying, I gave up, frustrated and now beginning to entertain the thought that maybe there was something wrong with my baby.

I wanted to talk to Nathan's doctor right away but the next appointment was two weeks away. I waited impatiently for the day to arrive. On the day of the visit I took Nathan in armed with all my notes of everything I observed that was 'wrong', and anxious for some assurances to give me peace of mind. My first appointment was with the outpatient clinic at UHWI. My sister Jennifer accompanied me on the visit and we went to the clinic sure that I would get some answers. The doctor who attended to us, however, was not on the same page. The wait was a long one and the registration process tedious. Finally after about two and a half hours it was our time to see the doctor. I entered a small room, rather impersonal and bare. I made a mental note of the space and thought to myself what a dull place to see babies. I had expected more light, colour and life in the room. But it was drab and dreary and gave me the impression that I would not get the answers I was seeking. The doctor said, "Good morning," and invited us to sit. Before my bottom hit the chair he started reeling off questions asking me for all of the birthing history from my previous pregnancies through to my pregnancy with Nathan. I answered the questions to the best of my rememberance all the time wondering what this had to do with our visit. The doctor noted my responses. He then went on to a second wave of questioning this time asking a specific set of 'prepared' questions about Nathan's day to day living. He made notes as I responded. I noted with growing interest that none of the questions he asked were about matters that I, as the parent, was concerned with. But I thought that this was routine and I would get the opportunity to ask my questions.

After a while the barrage of questions came to a halt. I saw it as my opportunity to now ask the questions from my list. So I told him that I had some questions and concerns. I shared them with him. He half listened and when I was done he said, "Mother, you have to understand that this baby is very sick. I am setting his next clinic appointment for six weeks. Please give this to the nurse outside (he handed me a file), and she will set the appointment." And just like that, he was done with us.

I left the clinic that day feeling such an acute sense of frustration, helplessness and that we were only a number and he (the doctor) didn't really care. I was no closer to understanding what was going on than when I first went in, and going there that day seemed like a colossal waste of my time.

I felt like it was a second strike. The hospital had failed us when my son was being discharged when they didn't inform us that the trauma my child had gone through had now put him in the high risk category for developing delays which could lead to a disability. This first clinic was a second opportunity for this to be corrected. Instead, it became a 'record-keeping' exercise and I left nowhere closer to understanding what I could possibly be dealing with or what I could do.

What made this such a pivotal point is if we had been given this information support early, there is a strong possibility that Nathan would not wear his disability to the extent that he wears it today. The very system that helped to save his life, and did a great job at doing so, had dropped the baton... twice!

Nathan's next appointment was to his private paedi-atrician for his four months well-baby check up and shots. This time I shared my concerns with his doctor. The doctor noted them and paid special attention to the lag in development. Nathan was developmentally delayed on almost every milestone with the exception of height – he was tall for his age. Developmental delay is when a child does not reach his or her developmental milestones at the expected times. It is an ongoing major or minor delay in the process of development. When a child is temporarily lagging behind, that is not called developmental delay. Delay can occur in one or many areas – for example, gross or fine motor, language, social or thinking skills.[1] There are many different types of developmental delays in infants and young children, these include problems with language or speech, vision, movement/motor skills, social and emotional skills, and thinking – cognitive skills. Sometimes, a delay occurs in many or all of these

areas, when that happens, it is called 'global developmental delay'.

Now I know the doctors knew all this. They also knew
the reasons that global developmental delay may
occur – a genetic defect such as Down's syndrome,
fetal alcohol syndrome caused by a mother drinking
alcohol during pregnancy, fragile X syndrome, an
inherited type of cognitive impairment, or severe
medical problems developing soon after birth often
associated with prematurity or in my son's case major
trauma caused by his congenital condition, surgery
and battle for his life. Doctors also know that warning
signs for different types of delays are most likely to
show up from infancy to age two. Yet no precautions
were taken to watch Nathan for signs of delays or to
educate me in what to look out for.

While developmental delay is most often a diagnosis
made by a doctor based on strict guidelines, research
informs that it is usually the parent who is the first to
notice that their child is not progressing at the same
rate as other children the same age. This was the case
for Nathan, and while the doctors from the UHWI post
surgery clinic ignored my concerns I could tell that

his private paediatrician was concerned. However, Nathan was technically still under the care of the UHWI and so the doctor deferred to the hospital. However, he did share with us that because Nathan had been through such a major and invasive trauma at birth and following, it was not unexpected that he may have some developmental delays. He spoke at length about the impact of trauma on a newborn's development and felt that with time Nathan might catch up. He said that if the UHWI felt the need to wait, and since he did not have access to Nathan's birth and surgery records, he would also wait. He did, however, put us on a more regular schedule of visits and told me the things to watch for so that we could map Nathan's development from then on. This made me feel a little better – but I was lulled into a false sense of hope.

Raising Nathan

Chapter 15

*Early Identification: Screening,
Assessment and Evaluation*

The first three years of a child's life are an
amazing time of development... and what
happens during those years stays with the child
for their lifetime. That's why it's so important to watch
for signs of delays in development, and to get help if
a problem is suspected. I have come to learn that the
sooner a child who is delayed gets early intervention,
the better their progress will be. In a perfect world
parents of young children would be empowered with
this information about children's development and
where there are concerns, for them to act early. I hold
the view that most parents look forward to the 'firsts'
in their child's development – first smile, first steps,
first words etc. So my question is, if this phase of
development is so critical, why is it that in some
countries appropriate attention is not given?
Wouldn't it make sense that programmes would be
in place to make use of this time? In the long run,
would it not be cheaper for a country to invest in

early development of children rather than to address the results of the deficits when a child gets older?

I came to learn, after the fact, that Jamaica was one of the countries that was still lagging in this area. I remember having a conversation with one of my sisters who is a nurse on a delivery ward in a hospital in the United States. Nathan was about three years old at the time and she asked me what early screening and intervention programme Nathan had received after he was discharged from the hospital at 24 days old. I told her none. For a moment, she being a Jamaican who had migrated to the United States in her early 20s and had been there for more than 25 years, could not believe that no referral was made. She told me that in the United States once a baby or young child had undergone any kind of trauma, that child was placed on a 'high risk' alert and was tracked for years to come for any early warning signs of delay. As part of the tracking process the child would undergo regular evaluations and would at the same time be given early intervention to mitigate any delays that may be developing.

I sat back when she dropped that bombshell and exclaimed, "Wow!" I was not aware that there was any such approach in Jamaica. I began to do some research and learned that she wasn't exaggerating. In the United States and Canada, for example, such attention is actually the norm. There was indeed coordinated national and localized efforts to encourage healthy child development – universal developmental and behavioural screening for children who are considered at risk – and support for the families and providers who care for them. Had my son been born in one of these countries he would have gotten this type of access as a normal course of action... which might have produced a different outcome for him.

The promotion of universal assessment is a major strategy for many countries around the world. The standard early assessment programme includes regular screenings to help raise awareness of a child's development, making it easier for parents and others caring for the child to know what to expect, what to look for and enable them to celebrate developmental milestones. These include hearing and vision screenings, and developmental and behavioural assessments to track a child's progress in areas such as language and social or motor development. This process serves to identify possible delays and concerns early, and to recommend the corrective course or helpful treatments. These processes also assist families, teachers and other professionals to ensure that babies and young children get the services and support they need as early as possible that will help them to thrive alongside their peers.

This was the opposite of our experience!

While I came to learn that Jamaica had a dearth of the requisite professionals and programmes in this area, there were several early stimulation intervention programmes, including two which were operated by the government – Early Stimulation/Stimulation Plus, and Rural Services for Persons with Disabilities. Several non-governmental organizations also ran programmes, including 3D Projects, Jamaica's first fully established community based rehabilitation programme focussing on three major areas of disability – sensory, learning and motor – and three crucial areas of rehabilitation – social, educational and economic. Either by negligence or ignorance, none of this information was given to me at any stage of the journey.

Instead they opted to gamble with my child's future and his life. They opted to wait and see how things turned out. At that time I was an uninformed parent. My faith in the doctors and specialists was so great that I never thought to question their decisions nor did I think to do any research. I was confident that my son was getting the best care and that these medical professionals would tell us what we needed to do each step of the way. So I drew my cue from the doctors and took on the posture of waiting.

Raising Nathan

Chapter 16
Back to Work

The day finally arrived, albeit too quickly, when I returned to work. It was one of the toughest decisions I've ever had to make. On the one hand I was glad to return to the safety and familiarity of my professional life, to get back into the thick of things. I loved my career and had missed it during the months that I was off. I felt like it was the only space where I was seen as myself. At work I was no one's mother or wife... I was just me. Don't get me wrong I am not ungrateful for the many blessings in my life. I love being married and being a mom. I love having a family of my own. I also just love being Christine and in my professional space I get to be just that. I could leave my problems at home (or so I thought) and for those blissful hours of work I could deal with the simpler things of life. The things I knew about and how to do... the things over which I had control. So maybe work was a blessing in disguise.

Raising Nathan

On the other hand Nathan was more behind in his development than ever and I was afraid for him. I knew in my heart that he wasn't okay and he needed me – my maternal-self longed to stay at home and take care of him. While we had taken great care to screen and hire someone who was competent to look after him, I was not convinced that I was doing the right thing. I tossed the pros and cons back and forth...

This was one of the first times that the lack of support surfaced. I wish I had someone with whom I could vacillate with this dilemma, someone who was neutral. It was a difficult topic to broach with family members who felt they were looking out for our interest and keeping us focused on the full picture. The question that was constantly raised was if I was to give up my job how would we manage financially? Common sense and economics won out – we were a two-income family and we needed the money, so with a sad heart I went back to work. It was bittersweet.

My first days back on the job were particularly long and difficult, largely because I couldn't keep focused. My body was at work but my heart and mind were at home. I was torn and didn't know how to fix it. As the days progressed I became more and more unhappy. I had lost my drive and fire and for the first time in my career I was just going through the motions at work. I must have phoned home every hour on the hour. And when I wasn't calling, I was thinking about Nathan. Every time my desk phone rang I jumped expecting that the call was an emergency to tell me that something was wrong at home. Thankfully it never was and the days gradually moved into weeks.

I had gained quite a bit of weight from the whole ordeal and I went back to work much heavier than I was pre-pregnancy. Normally I would hit the gym within six weeks of delivery and within six months would have shed most of the baby weight. Going to the gym was usually my way to refocus on me. This was not the case this time and even though my company paid for gym membership and I had signed up, I could not motivate myself to engage in something so trivial. I rushed home from work each evening to see Nathan – and he was always the same way as I had left him, there was no change. Each evening I would stifle a tear at the ensuing disappointment that my son was not getting better – he seemed to be getting worse.

Raising Nathan

As the weeks went by Nathan's under-development became more and more evident. He was now six months old and had not learned to sit up even if he was being propped up. He had not learned to lift his head and so when he was carried his neck rolled over backwards and lagged behind him – something he should have mastered by about four to six weeks old. He still could not roll over – even with help his arms and legs would get stuck when he tried as if he lacked the strength to correct himself. The fisting of his hands had become more pronounced and when he grasped an object he held it in a pincher's grasp – a very basic movement. His floppiness had become worse to the point that I was sometimes afraid to hold him for fear he would slip out of my arms.

Visually he did not seem able to fix his gaze on anything. As we tried to get his attention with brightly coloured and noisy toys he would turn his head to the side when an item was presented to him. It was later that we learned that he was using his peripheral vision. Peripheral vision in simple language is side vision, and is the ability to see objects and movement from outside of the direct line of vision.[1] Nathan was not able to use his central vision and so looked at everything from the side – and he was partial to his right side. He also had difficulty focusing and could not track an item moving at any speed across his line of vision. Of all these the most disheartening for me was that he did not seem to recognize or be aware of the world around him and was unresponsive to stimuli such as smiling or waving. He also did not react to any sounds which again brought his hearing into question. The only sound he made was when he cried and even then it was a slight sound as his lung capacity was still weak.

The delays persisted through six months, seven months. It was at the seven month point that I drew the line. By this time I had made two other visits to the outpatient clinic at UHWI before abandoning that route. It was just a glorious 'record-taking' experience and a grand waste of our time. I scheduled an appointment with Nathan's paediatrician resolute that I would not leave his office until he had accepted that something was wrong and given us a referral to see a specialist.

I began to notice a change in the paediatrician – I could tell that he was growing concerned. It was now that I learned the importance of parents' attentiveness to every detail of their child's development. I came to understand that although each baby develops in his or her own individual way and at his or her own rate, failure to reach certain developmental milestones may be early warning signs of medical or developmental problems. I also found out that the 'wait and see' approach is not the best strategy, as the majority of delays do not go away on their own but often require specific intervention and support... and the earlier, the better. Some of the telling 'red flags' that alerted us that Nathan was in trouble were:

- He didn't seem to hear or respond to loud sounds at any distance from him.

- He didn't take any notice of his hands or any of his body parts for that matter. At times when his hands would pop up before his face he appeared startled and didn't seem to know what they were.

- He didn't smile when he was smiled at or at the sound of my voice, his dad's voice or his siblings' voices.

- He didn't follow or track moving objects with his eyes.

- He could not grasp and hold objects.

- He could not hold his head upright.

And all of this was further compounded with the reflux issue which still persisted. Nathan kept throwing up even after drinking an ounce of juice. Drinking water was also very difficult for him.

I struggled at work. I still loved the job but I was out of my mind with worry. The whole experience had taken its toll on me. I stopped smiling. As the days went by I could tell that some of my co-workers were becoming increasingly uncomfortable around me. I could see in the eyes of many of them that they wanted to help but didn't know how and I was too wrapped up in my pain to know how I needed to be helped. After a while I began to avoid social settings within the work environment. I did my work, kept to myself and went home. But this social isolation made me feel even worse as I felt that I should be swapping new baby stories and showing pictures. I did not even have a picture of Nathan in my wallet.

Raising Nathan

While so many things seemed to have been going wrong with Nathan's development there were things which were going right. We were at home one Saturday morning. I was sitting on the couch watching TV in the living room, the central pulse of our home. Robert was off somewhere else in the house and all the kids were on the floor playing with Nathan. He had just been given a baby activity gym with coloured dangling mobiles in shapes and farm animals. Adrianne, Jordanne and Ryan, who were fascinated with this new toy, were trying to get Nathan to play with it. Unexpectedly Jordanne exclaimed loudly. She jumped up and ran to me and said, "Mommy, mommy, now Nathan looks like a person." Caught by surprise with her statement but curious nonetheless I asked her what she meant. She replied, "Look, see, he now has eyelashes and hair over his eyes." I stared at his face in amazement and she was right! I had thought that his face looked a little strange when he was in the hospital and when he came home. But I had not realized that I had not examined Nathan like I had following the birth of each of my other children. When they were each handed to me I had examined their little faces – two eyes, one nose, one mouth, two ears; and bodies – ten fingers, ten toes, etc. In Nathan's case, not getting the chance to hold him at birth had denied me that close up look. His days in the hospital didn't improve matters and by the time he did come home, all I saw was how sick he was and the wound from the surgery. I bent down and looked into his little face and I saw what Jordanne meant. I ran to get one of his early pictures and held it up to his face. In it he did not have eyelashes nor eyebrows and barely any hair on his head. While we had been focusing on what was not going well I had missed what was going right. Nathan had begun to thrive in his own way! He had grown enviable long black silky eye-lashes, and two beautifully luscious and well contoured eyebrows! His face no longer looked strange. He had grown a beautiful cherubic face. Though this was no big deal because I loved my child anyway, I felt like it was a small win. At least there was now one thing that was going right. Nathan's eyes grew into dancing eyes, his luxurious eyelashes and eyebrows remain one of his most beautiful and compelling features even to this day. Each time I look into his eyes I am reminded of that day...

It was my first step into learning to look for and celebrate every accomplishment, big or small, because each is a gift from God.

Raising Nathan

As the days went on, however, this lesson became buried back in the sea of despair as everyone around us made it a habit to point out what Nathan couldn't do – as though I did not have eyes to see for myself. This fed my uneasiness which grew with each passing day until I could no longer bury the surety that something was definitely wrong.

Chapter 17

The Defining Moment

I once read that in every life there is a defining moment... that moment in time when we cross an invisible line that changes our course and trajectory. Sometimes we get to a crossroads in life and know that our next choice will change our course. But I believe that some of our most profoundly defining moments are serendipitous. We are not conscious of that invisible line and we step over it and it is not until much later when we stop to take stock of where we are and we ask ourselves how we got here, that we can trace that moment back to a specific time and a specific choice or action.

I believe that the day I became pregnant with Nathan was my first defining moment that would lead to a new course and direction for my life. At each step of the way I had a choice in how I would view what was happening to me. I could have drowned myself in sorrow, dejection and shut down. But there was a spirit inside of me that didn't see that as a viable option.

Raising Nathan

Please don't get me wrong, I am not in any way trivializing or condemning persons who become overwhelmed by the circumstances. I am simply trying to explain the wars that waged inside of me and still continue to this day. What I began to do unsuspectingly was to fight one battle at a time and make one decision at a time.

We were now at the seventh month marker. This was the marker the paediatrician had given to see if Nathan would catch up. He had not. His developmental delays were now very significant and new signs were emerging almost daily. We had a Saturday morning appointment to see the paediatrician. The evening before I was at home, zoned out in front of the television. It was about 9:30pm, Robert was still at work and the children were all asleep. I was determined not to worry or become obsessed about what the visit the next day would reveal. I was flipping channels when a story caught my attention. My first introduction to the story was the image of a little boy about five or so years old who was sitting in the biggest stroller I had ever seen. There was a young woman with him, who presumably was his mother, and she was talking in an interview about the difficult turn their lives had taken because of her son's diagnosis. The words caught my attention and something deep inside told me that I needed to pay attention. So I quietened my inside and actively listened to what she was saying. She said her son was diagnosed with 'zerebraal pawlsy', I had never heard of the term before. As a matter of fact I had only heard of autism and so I listened. She shared how her life changed with her son's diagnosis and how she had to quit her job to care for him. She shared all the places she had to take him daily to get the help he needed. As I watched and listened she turned and looked directly into my eyes and spoke to me about what she has had do to help her son and how she has to advocate and lobby for support. I felt in my heart that this was God speaking to me and preparing me and that my son had whatever her son had. I listened until I heard the interviewer repeat the words 'cerebral palsy'. The close caption on the television set spelled the words and I read it a couple of times, before running for a pen to write it down.

The next morning we arrived at the doctor's office on time for our appointment. I went with Nathan alone and Robert stayed home with the other children. After a brief check the doctor turned to face me and said, "Mrs Ebanks, as I suspected all these months your son is delayed. He is now at seven months old exhibiting wide-reaching/global developmental delays brought on by what I believe is a condition called cerebral palsy." He paused to look at me searching my face for a reaction. I said to him, "Doc, I know." I stared at him stony-eyed as he shared what he knew. He had been doing some research because he was not at that time familiar with the condition, all he could give was a prognosis. He then told me that he was referring Nathan to a paediatric neurologist for a diagnosis. He handed me a referral letter and we took our leave.

I felt numb as I drove home. I felt I had nothing else to give. I was out of tears, in grief beyond imagination. It was as if he had just told me that my child was dying. I had no clue what cerebral palsy was but it felt like a death sentence. I also noticed the look of pity in the doctor's eyes and I felt sorry for my baby. I drove silently home and when I was nearing the house realized that I was not ready to face my husband. How could I look at him and tell him our child... God's gift to us... was broken?

I telephoned Robert on his mobile phone and he answered on the first ring. I knew that he must have
been on edge waiting to hear the outcome of the visit,
but I couldn't face him... not yet. I asked him to meet
me at the gate to collect Nathan in his carry seat. He
said okay and didn't ask me anything. I was grateful. I
arrived home and handed a sleeping Nathan to him
without a word. Without looking back I drove off. I
had no destination in mind I just needed to clear my
head and I needed to talk to God. I was confused.
When I had the premonition when I was newly pregnant
I was sure I had heard that this child was to have been
a gift from God, and with this child I would prove God;
hence my confusion. How could God give me a gift that
was broken?

I drove around for a while. I don't know how long
I drove. I could not think, could not feel, I was just
numb and confused at the same time. How could this
have happened? What did I do wrong? What does all
of this mean? Like opening a floodgate the questions
poured out. After a while I parked by the side of the
road rested my head on the steering wheel and wept.
I prayed. "Lord, I know you are ever present and that
you are All-Wise and All-Knowing. You heard what

the doctor said just now. I don't even know how I am supposed to feel, or what to say to Robert. I don't know why you have allowed this and my heart is breaking for my poor, poor child. What are we going to do? Help me Lord, help us through this." I cried some more and when I was spent, I wiped my tears started the car and pointed it in the direction for home. It was time to break the news to my husband.

Nathan was asleep when I got home. It was hours later and our other children were playing somewhere in the house totally oblivious that our lives were forever changed... again. I sat in front of Robert and he looked at me waiting. It is in times of difficulty that you notice the little things. Things like whenever I had bad news Robert always seemed to know. He would sit and look at me patiently waiting for me to say what I had to say. I opened my mouth and everything just spilled out. I was telling him everything all at once crying and praying all at the same time. Robert listened in his usual quiet way and let me talk uninterrupted. When I stopped he took my hand in his and said softly, "Honey, this is our child. We will love him and care for him no matter what. Don't worry, we will figure this out together. It will be alright, I promise." I never loved my husband more and for the first time since I received the news I felt a surge of hope. We spoke for a while longer and made arrangements to go and see the neurologist together and then I went to take a nap. It had been a physically and emotionally exhausting day and I was drained.

In the months since he was born I had seen my baby go from one crisis to another. I never had the chance to experience the new-baby-coming-home feeling, that a mother gets as she watches her little miracle adjust to life in the world, and that I had been privileged to experience with each of my other three children. From the get go, it felt like anything that could go wrong had gone wrong. I was shock-weary and tired of all the developments and resulting disappointments. I did not choose any of this nor did I bargain for any of it. I felt like I was caught up in someone else's nightmare, or that someone made some really bad decisions on my behalf and didn't bother to tell me. When would this bad news end? In that moment I felt a wave of despair so great that I felt like it was consuming me. I felt like throwing my hands into the air and giving up. I had come to another crossroads. The same spirit that was in me from the first day I felt I was pregnant and had surfaced at every intersection of decision, surfaced again. Like the character 'Dorothy' in one of my favorite childhood movies the 'Wizard of Oz' I needed to follow the yellow brick road to see where the trail ended. I needed to keep moving forward.

We were 'fortunate' to receive an appointment with the neurologist four weeks from that day. And so I resolved to do some research so that I would not go into the meeting high and dry. It also made me feel useful that I was doing something to help my child. In those moments I again wished that there was someone or some place I could go to help me organize my thoughts. I thought that if I at least was able to pronounce the name it would make me sound like I was a hands-on parent. So I practiced day and night, saying over and over and over again – 'seh-ree-brul pawl-zee'.[1]

We were now at step one in the new phase of our journey. Healthychildren.org defines a pediatric or child neurologist as a medical specialist who combines the special expertise in diagnosing and treating disorders of the nervous system (brain, spinal cord, muscles, nerves) with an understanding of medical

disorders in childhood and the special needs of
the child and his or her family and environment.
Ordinarily the child neurologist works in a team with
pediatricians or other primary care doctors in addition
to other pediatric specialists to care for children who
have more complex or serious medical issues, such as
birth defects, intellectual disability or as in our case
cerebral palsy. [2]

As the day of the appointment drew closer the prognosis of cerebral palsy obscured my child completely.
When I looked at Nathan all I saw was 'seh-ree-
brul pawl-zee'. We went to the appointment and met
the doctor. He was a frail man but very imposing. It
felt like he was sitting up on a 'judgement throne' and
we were at the foot of his throne. He was aloof, clinical
and seemingly inhuman. He scared me. He asked the
questions expecting only yes or no answers. At times
when I interjected with an anecdote to explain the
answer to one of his questions he would utter, "Mrs
Ebanks, I did not ask you for a diagnosis just answer
the question." At no point did I feel that he saw us as
human beings, it felt like my child was a diagnosis
and that first appointment was only to collect our
case history.

Raising Nathan

After what felt like an eternity the initial meeting was over. And here is the shocker. We paid heartily for the visit but I left the appointment with a referral for a Computerized Axial Tomography (CAT) scan of Nathan's brain, some blood tests and no closer understanding of what was wrong with my child. I dared to ask the doctor what was 'seh-ree-brul pawl-zee'. His response (word indecipherable) was to leave the diagnosis to him.

The CAT scan was the first neuroimaging test we were asked to take. For those who may thankfully never have run-ins with this bad boy, the CAT scan combines a series of X-ray views taken from many different angles and computer processing to create cross-sectional images of the bones and soft tissues inside the body. In Nathan's case the test was necessary to look at his brain so as to rule out other conditions such as infections in and around the brain (encephalitis or meningitis), evaluate large or increasing head size, or screen for a build-up of excess cerebrospinal fluid in the brain at birth (congenital hydrocephalus).

Nathan was more than his usual squirmy self that day and the technician got the long arm of Nathan's misbehaving. Luckily for Nathan once he pulled out his secret weapon, his 'million-dollar smile' all was forgiven. After a long and tiresome wait Nathan quietened down to regain his energy and the test was carried out.

The results weren't so great for the CAT scan. It reported:

Clinical Details: *Global developmental delays.*
NCCT Brain: *Mild generalized cerebral atrophy is noted. The gyri are large and broad based most notably over the frontal lobe. The ventricles, basal cisterns and extra axial areas are enlarged in keeping with the degree of atrophy. No intracranial hemorrhage is seen.*
Impression: *Generalized cerebral atrophy. Findings suggestive of pachygyria.*

I had by then made it my duty to request a copy of whatever tests we ran on Nathan. So when I received my copy I raced home to the medical dictionary. What is cerebral atrophy? I am so glad you asked. The definition I found from the National Institute of Neurological Disorders and Strokes states that:

'Cerebral atrophy is a common feature of many of the diseases that affect the brain. Atrophy of any tissue means loss of cells. In brain tissue atrophy describes a loss of neurons and the connections between them. Atrophy can be generalized which means that all of the brain has shrunk; or it can be local affecting only a limited area of the brain and resulting in a decrease of the functions that area of the brain controls. If the cerebral hemispheres (the two lobes of the brain that form the cerebrum) are affected, conscious thought and voluntary processes may be impaired.'[3]

In Nathan's case what the test showed was that he had cerebral palsy in which lesions (damaged areas) had impaired his motor coordination. It didn't just stop there but got worse... 'Cerebral atrophy is also associated with dementia, seizures and a group of language disorders called the aphasias.'[3] I froze at seizures (epilepsy). I panicked but kept on reading. 'Seizures can take different forms, appearing as disorientation, repetitive movements, loss of consciousness or convulsions.'[3] "Oh Lord," I thought, "Can it get any worse?"

I quickly typed 'pachygyria' in my web browser:

> *'Pachygyria (from the Greek 'pachy' meaning 'thick' or 'fat' gyri) is a congenital malformation of the cerebral hemisphere. It results in unusually thick convolutions of the cerebral cortex. Typically children have developmental delay and seizures, the onset and severity depending on the severity of the cortical malformation. Infantile spasms are common in affected children, as is intractable epilepsy.'*[4]

I was done researching. It was time to pull out the big artillery... It was time to pray. I got down on my knees by my bed and spread out the report on the bed. I prayed, "Father in heaven, this is what man has to say, what do you say?" I now firmly knew that matters were totally out of my hands and solidly in the hands of God.

I dropped off the results to the neurologist the following day. We met with him for the follow up appointment the following week. This was when he delivered the diagnosis. Our son had cerebral palsy. Funnily by that time I could pronounce the words flawlessly – *cerebral palsy*.

Chapter 18

And My Child Grew More and More Invisible Each Day

Interestingly when I didn't know what was going on, I thought that was the worst it could get. But I was wrong. The diagnosis ushered in a new dimension of the unknown, of worry and fear. Each day my son, the child, became more and more invisible as the diagnosis took his place. Before long I lost sight of my child. All of my conversations became about his diagnosis. I would run into someone who knew I had been pregnant but didn't know the details and they would ask how the baby was and I would launch into a chronicle of his diagnosis.

It didn't help that all of our visits with the neurologist after that were about the disability, never the child. This affected my view of my son. Each day as I cared for him I did not see a baby, I saw cerebral palsy. It was as if a blight had descended on our household. Even our other children sensed that something was wrong. Robert and I barely had time to talk. We were on opposite ends trying to keep our family moving forward. We both put in long hours at work. We came home and went through the newly evolving routine of caring for a child with special needs. Just like that and without warning, we had become 'one of those families' – we had become a special needs family.

I buried myself in my work to stop myself from thinking about the situation. I felt very sorry for myself, angry and embarrassed. And I felt deep pity for my poor, poor baby. What was to become of him? I wished there was someone I could talk to, someone who wouldn't look at me with pity, someone who would know the right thing to say, someone who had been there before and understood what I couldn't even articulate. But there was no one. So I kept it all bottled up, saved for the occasions when I spilled to a few close friends. I tried not to do that much because I saw their discomfort as they did not know what to say or how to help me. This isolated me even further.

Of the two of us I think Robert was hardest hit. I can only imagine the difficulty of a father seeing his son going through this, and he being a loving, caring and overly protective dad, knowing there was nothing he could do.

And My Child Grew More and
More Invisible Each Day

Unlike me, Robert didn't have close friends and so he had no one to talk to. I watched him get up every day, his shoulders a little more hunched over than the day before, new signs of grey hairs which had come in prematurely as he carried his burden alone. Though I watched I wasn't doing great myself and so was not of much help to him. Oh how I wished in those moments that we had somewhere we could go, someone we could talk to, someone who cared and understood our grief. Someone who wouldn't judge us or tell us the empty words of "God knows best" – words we were not yet ready to listen to.

Nathan was nine months old before his neurologist finally referred us to a pediatric physiotherapist, Shandrel Saint.[1] Shandrel requested that we run an MRI test as she wanted to see whether the abnormal readings of the brain were due to bleeding on the brain. I prayed through the process. We took the test and the results came back negative, which was good!

Raising Nathan

Chapter 19

Learning to Cope

Looking back I realize now how bitter and hostile I had become. I was deeply defensive and found it difficult to maintain close relationships with people who had children of a similar age as my son. Although I was glad to see their children growing up it was difficult to see another baby thrive, develop and get into everything while mine lay flat on the floor, unable to sit or crawl, even at the age of two. I also felt angry when people thought they were qualified to tell me what I should and shouldn't do, or to say how marvelously I was coping. I felt neither marvelous nor that I was coping well. Furthermore it seemed that this was an indication of their view that my child was a burden. Privately I felt this way myself at times which I came to understand was all a fairly typical and predictable response, and part and parcel of adjusting to having a child with special needs.

Although I presented a bold front to those around me, the truth of the matter was that I was depressed, scared and dying on the inside. While I was fortunate to have a family which offered financial help, what I needed most was physical and emotional help. I wanted to talk about my child all of the time, and yet I didn't want to talk about the situation. I wanted someone to listen and not try to give me advice. I wanted a hug. I tried not to complain, however, because I knew that there were moms and dads who were not as lucky as we were because Robert and I had each other, so we were not alone.

Then I got an unexpected gift from a co-worker named Dawn. We had met briefly when she had worked on a function I had organized and every once in a while she would phone me. I don't know what made her call one day when I was at my desk and at my lowest. The phone rang and I picked it up and she was on the other end. She had this very bubbly personality and infectious laughter and within moments of our conversation my mood lifted. We spoke a bit about work and then she asked me the dreaded question: how was Nathan? I shared with her candidly for a few minutes before catching myself. To my relief she asked why I had stopped talking and told me to continue because she wanted to hear. She listened to me as if there was nothing else and no one else in the world. That day a very special friendship started. A friendship that was to journey with me for several years and would help me to deepen my faith and affirm what I was doing to help my son.

The days and weeks following the diagnosis were the most difficult. Though the cerebral palsy was not yet defined, the diagnosis had come as a terrible blow and threw my world into disarray. I was devastated and so confused that I recall little else about those first days other than the heartbreak. I have since read how one parent described this event as 'a black sack being pulled down over her head, blocking her ability to hear, see and think in normal ways'. Another parent described the trauma as having a 'knife stuck in her heart'.[1] This may seem overly dramatic to someone who has not had this experience but to quote an old proverb, 'Don't judge a man until you have walked a mile in his shoes'. Loosely translated it means you should not judge someone until you know exactly how they feel or why they are doing something. Having been there I understand exactly what they mean, but even these words may not sufficiently describe the rampaging flood of emotions that assail the heart, mind and life of a parent who has learnt that their child has a disabling condition.

My situation was compounded at work by there having been three of us who were pregnant at the same time. Nathan was the second to be born and the only one born with a challenge and who developed a challenge. I stopped talking about him because I had grown tired of people telling me that they were sorry to hear about his condition. I know they meant well but it made me feel worse about our predicament.

The diagnosis was step two in our new journey and the weeks following were very burdensome. Once the diagnosis had been made and before I could draw breath, we were launched into a flurry of tests, observations, tests, screenings and more tests to confirm the diagnosis and identify the cause. The next six months were a precarious balancing dance of work, family and the battery of appointments. At times I felt that if a feather was dropped on top of all we were carrying I would keel over. Now these tests weren't simple tests, they were tests that required a child diagnosed with a movement disorder and incessant writhing to stay absolutely still for an inordinately long time – a mission impossible for Nathan.

Because cerebral palsy is a neuro disorder we learned the hard way that once Nathan becomes excited, agitated or angry, movement erupts from every appendage on his body making him difficult to control – often disastrous for the well-being of those who get in the way of his arms, legs and head. If he is excited enough he will also pinch, a skill that we celebrated as bittersweet. For while pinching is a fine motor skill and noted developmental milestone, unfortunately Nathan was like any other kid and when he was angry it became a weapon, and to put it in Jamaican parlance 'him pinch hat!' There have been times when I was one of his unfortunate victims and had to fight the strong urge to pinch him back. He did not get off so easily with his siblings!

My need for more knowledge grew with every passing experience and I started to realize that if I was going to be of any use or support to my son, if I did not want him to go the way I had seen so many children with disabilities go, trapped in limbo because of a lack of the services they needed and poor expectations of them, then I had to get moving with the decision to quit my job. This was much harder than I had imagined however, because if there was ever a time we needed two incomes, the time was then.

Over the next months I threw myself into work as I searched for the right time to make the move. I needed to take my mind off my problems. I remember someone once told me that when you have troubles of your own, you should find someone to help. This releases the stress of your own problems and sometimes the distance helps to give you a better perspective. I tried that, but it didn't work. I was unhappy, torn and had a feeling of helplessness which I couldn't shake. Nathan was still very behind and despite my faithfulness to carry out test after test and make every specialist appointment, nothing was changing. He was being more and more delayed, and I still knew very little about how to manage his condition.

As Nathan moved through toddlerhood the impact of his condition became more manifest and worrisome. His body was still very limp and when I held him his body did not contract or engage, he just lay in my arms passively. None of his survival reflexes worked. If you sat him up with cushions and he toppled forward, he would fall smack onto his face if you didn't catch him in time. His neck was weak and his head lolled from side to side because of the weight. Every attempt to roll on the ground caused his head to slam into the floor with what became a too familiar sound of cranium and skin connecting forcefully with a tough surface. As a result we constantly hovered over him – his grandparents still get flustered and agitated when he bangs his head today.

Nathan was never left alone for fear of him hurting himself and somewhere along the way the little genius began to use this to his advantage! When he wanted to escape something he didn't like, whether therapy or school, he would bang his head and then look at you with command-performance tears which he seemed to be able to summon just like that. When he turned seven, I began to wean him off always having someone with him, in order grow his independence, but he didn't like it one bit and that stubborn streak, the same streak with which he fought for life, has grown much stronger over the years, and is resisting it. I started with baby steps, leaving him alone for two to four minutes at a time, progressing to 25–30 minutes, now

Raising Nathan

he makes it through an entire 90 minute movie on his own before you hear the telltale signs of being summoned.

Chapter 20
Debunking the Myths

Disabled Peoples' International *states that myths, stereotypes and stigma about disability are barriers to the realization of the human rights of people with disabilities.*

E arlier I introduced the topic of common myths, misconceptions and misunderstanding about disabilities. The Ontario Ministry of Community and Social Services aptly described myths about disabilities as 'Roadblocks that interfere with the ability of persons with disabilities to have equality in employment.' In the case of children with disabilities, these roadblocks can severely impair their own parents and family's view and treatment of the child. These myths, misconceptions usually result from a lack of the correct information, experience and interaction with persons with disabilities. This lack of familiarity has nourished negative attitudes which have erected barriers for persons with disabilities. It's important to learn the facts to remove these roadblocks and to stop discrimination. I have dedicated this chapter to addressing some of the common myths and facts about people with disabilities.

Myth: **'A person's disability defines who they are as an individual.'** People often label individuals with a disability according to their condition or limitations. It is common in our daily lives to hear references such as 'disabled' or 'epileptic'. I want to make a statement that persons with disabilities are people first, their disability or ability does not define them. I will deal with this issue in more details in a later chapter, but would like to share a slogan I found and like, 'Label Jars, Not People'.

Myth: **'People with disabilities are sick and in constant pain.'** I cannot even begin to count the number of times people, some of them 'well-meaning' have referred to my son as being sick, or ask, "How is your sick child?" I would like to make the point that people, whether children or adults with disabilities, are like people without disabilities. They get sick on occasion with a cold, or flu, or some other ailment like everyone else. Generally, unless the disability is something like

Rheumatoid arthritis which some children do get early in life, people with disabilities typically do not suffer or experience pain due to their condition. And just in case you are wondering, no, Nathan does not suffer pains due to cerebral palsy.

Myth: This next myth is one I hear a lot and it says: **'Disability is a personal tragedy and deserves our pity.'** Disability is often viewed as an unending burden. People with disabilities are often viewed as tragic figures on whom society should have pity. An influential person once told me that disability is and will always be charity. He could not see any value that persons with disabilities could contribute. Disability does not mean a poor quality of life. It is often the negative attitudes of society and the lack of accessibility within the community that are the real tragedy.

Nathan may have a disability but he is by no means fragile or helpless. He uses whatever he has at his disposal to voice his displeasure or pleasure. He smiled actively for the first time at about nine months old (though his neurologist tried to refute this calling it a spasm). But I know that he looked in my eyes and smiled. But because I was so caught up with finding a

'fix' or a 'cure' for Nathan and I saw him as 'broken',
I did not pay attention to his strengths, particularly
his charm. Like all of us when we find an attribute,
Nathan groomed his smile. He has a smile that makes
everyone go, "Aahhh," a smile that makes everyone smile
back at him. I remember one occasion in particular when
his smile put me in a very uncomfortable position. I
had taken him for his first hearing assessment at the
Caribbean Hearing Centre in Central Plaza, up-town
Kingston. We had been given a ride with my father-in-
law who had dropped us off and left when I told him
Robert was coming to join us. Robert was running late
at work and had not yet arrived after we were finished,
so I decided to go out into the car park to wait for him.

As we stood on the piazza, Nathan in his stroller looking
out, I saw in the corner of my eye a black car with
heavily tinted windows circle the driveway and then
pull up a short distance from us. At first I did not pay it
any attention until I saw the driver alight from the car
and heading in our general direction. I looked and saw
it was a gentleman and he looked so fierce and like he
was coming to hurt us that all the blood drained from
my legs and I could not move. As I played the scenario
over in my head as he approached, I started to wonder

what I had done and then thought that he must be coming to rob us. As he drew nearer I was working out my defence if he tried anything, of how I would club him with my walking-stick umbrella before I fled with Nathan. He walked right up and into my personal space so close that as he opened his mouth I could see my own reflection in his jade, gold and red 'false' teeth! Before I could react he bent down with a smile that looked more like a scowl and said to Nathan in a raspy sandpaper voice, "Waa gwaan rude bouy?" He touched Nathan's little hand gently before looking up at me and said, "Yuh fe tek care a him yuh 'ere?" I swallowed and nodded my head vigorously, grateful that it wasn't a daylight robbery as I had feared. He then turned and walked off in another direction. I bent down to see if Nathan was alright and saw the bait. What drew the man to us was that as he drove by Nathan had flashed him his million-dollar smile and compelled the man to come and say hi. As the man walked away, Nathan sat smiling like an angel, looking at his departing back. Nathan was now engaging with the world – and I was missing this phase because of my preoccupation with what was 'wrong' with him and what was 'different' about him.

Raising Nathan

Another strength that Nathan exhibited early on was that he had a good first impression assessment of people. I came to realize that anyone he didn't respond to was not a nice person to be around, and those he responded to were 'good' people. I learned this the hard way.

I hadn't noticed his reaction when we hired the first two live-in housekeepers. They didn't work out well for us as I discovered they were mean-spirited, unpleasant and difficult to get along with. Somewhere along the way I noted that Nathan didn't warm to the ladies either and so I tested my theory with the next person we hired. I interviewed the candidates and shortlisted them, and then during a final interview I would find a reason to ask them to hold Nathan for me for a second. His reaction was obvious right away. He refused to go to two of the candidates but smiled, cooed and went to the third without hesitation. She worked with us for two and a half years before moving on to other things. Nathan became a valuable stakeholder during the interviews and his judgment has never been wrong – everyone we chose this way ended up being a close friend of the family even after moving on to greener pastures.

As time went by I started to learn to celebrate the little steps. I had begun to learn more about cerebral palsy and came to recognize that outside of a miracle, which I believed could happen, his development was going to require specific intervention, time, energy and my input. I grew less angry and less desperate and began to settle into my role as the mother of a child with special needs. As my skills and knowledge increased so did my attitude. I felt empowered and as I did I also became less interested in looking for 'miracle pills' and more content to learn about the management of the condition.

I read everything. I don't remember what it is like reading for fun. Since Nathan's diagnosis all of my reading has been in the disability, special education, parenting and special needs fields. I have read hundreds of books, articles, reviews and blogs covering a wide range of topics in the field. The more I read the more I became dissatisfied with the level of care that Nathan was receiving as I began to learn that there were so many more services that he needed – and none of these services were available in Jamaica. What was I to do? I did not know anyone with the right knowledge and who didn't see my son as a 'client ticket' or as a broken instrument which needed to be fixed. My knowledge of his condition was growing exponentially but while I had a job I could not find enough time to explore what was out there. I began to feel a pressure from within to quit my full time job so that I could focus my time and energy on helping my son. I felt like I was running out of time. I did not yet know how significant that feeling was and that the window of significant brain development (zero to seven years) was rapidly closing.

Chapter 21

Life Gives You Lemons, Make Lemonade:
Building a New Game Plan

As the months progressed my discomfort grew with the way things were. Robert and I would stay up late at nights talking about what was happening. I would share what I had read and explain the deep calling I felt about the need to clear my schedule so I could be more available to learn, grow my knowledge and develop some advocacy skills to effectively help to direct the course of our son's development. It might have appeared to be a lofty ambition but deep down I felt that this was the reason for Nathan's birth, that he came into the world to open my eyes to the plight of so many children and families. I kept hearing my pastor's voice ringing out in my ears, "Anything that you are sick and tired about, it meant that God brought you here to do something about it." I was certainly sick and tired of the stagnant state of things. I was sick and tired that there was so little information and resources available to help me. I was sick and tired of the doom and gloom attitude of many of the specialists who worked with us. I was sick and

tired that Nathan still did not have any proper rehabilitation equipment and aids because these were not
available locally. I was fed up, sick and tired!

We had enrolled Nathan in a physical therapy programme
at nine months old which we faithfully followed twice
per week. I am sure the neighbours did not like us
much for these two years because they had to endure
an hour of screaming. Nathan liked the therapist but
hated the work and became very skilled at avoiding it.

Nathan was a selective listener. When his hearing was
tested on a number of occasions he did not indicate
that he heard the sounds that were played to him, yet
from as early as 15 months he would know when the
therapist's car pulled up at our gate because no matter
what he was doing, he would stop and begin to cry
and she would knock at the front door a few moments
later. No, he did not like therapy one bit and who could
blame him. Unfortunately for the therapist the stubborn
determination that kept him alive became his vice, and
he fought her tooth and nail.

Life Gives You Lemons, Make Lemonade:
Building a New Game Plan

There were days when Nathan was up, bright-eyed and bushy-tailed and so distracted in playing that he didn't hear her car pull up or know she had arrived until she walked into the living room. On one such occasion he was unbelievably silent as she went through the preparations – massage, stretching and strapping on a crudely made standing device. When she tried to get him to stand he was 'fast asleep' – not real sleep, but the sleep which says 'I am not really sleeping, but I am going to pretend I am until you stop bothering me and go away.' She had struggled in frustration until she finally gave up and left. And no sooner had her car pulled away from the gate than Nathan 'woke up' smiling, and looking like he got the last cookie from the cookie jar!

On another occasion when she didn't take his 'no' for an answer, Nathan got so angry that he grabbed at her head. He was in such a rage that his hands fisted up tightly and he yanked out a handful of her silky brown hair. It took us a while to calm him enough to loosen his grip. Needless to say for the rest of the time she came the therapist never wore her hair hanging down. I also believe this contributed significantly to her saying that she could not do anything else for him when

he got to 18 months. She said that he needed rehabilitation equipment and assistive aids which she did not
have, and recommended that we send him to the one
privately owned facility in Jamaica that catered for
children like my son.

I wasn't totally convinced that this was the right decision
– I was still caught up in the idea of being able to 'fix'
him, and the promise of more therapy was a strong
appeal and so we went along with her suggestion.

My first visit to the school was a day I will never forget.
Armed with the physiotherapist's recommendation
and Nathan's neurology report, I found the school. The
yard leading to the building was pleasant enough but
when I entered the building I was shocked. It was lit-
erally a wide open space and my first impression was
how dark the space was. The space was never intended for a school and so had poor lighting and ventila-
tion. The physical presentation was everything that I
abhorred in a child care facility.

It was not a typical school for there was no furniture.
Instead there were mats on the floor and the children,

many of them living with physical disabilities, were lying on the mats or sitting in their wheelchairs. It was depressing. Some of the children brought their own aids such as a standing device or walking device but the school had some homemade devices which it used with the other children. The programme was obviously underfunded.

Though I was taken aback when I saw the school I felt I had no other option. I took up the offer out of desperation. Nathan was only 18 months old when we enrolled him there.. The principal of the school told us that they generally do not take children before they are three but they made an exception for Nathan. I walked away that day feeling like I had let down my son, especially when I compared his school to the school his siblings attended. I felt that he deserved more than that but felt trapped because there was nowhere else to take him. I drove away and headed to his siblings' school where I parked my car and broke down in tears. "Lord, why does nobody care?" I asked. "These children deserve to be in pleasant, engaging classrooms. Look at where they are, it is so dark and uninviting, why doesn't anybody care about them?" As I sat in my car, the silence broken intermittently by

my sniffling, I heard a still small voice respond,
"I care."

Though the school is well known in Jamaica it is and
remains a very small school and at the time had an
enrolment of 20–25 children with various disabilities,
many of them multiple. I threw my energies into fundraising for the school using my corporate connections
to sell their Christmas cards and supporting other
fundraising to help enrich the facilities. I even got
my company to do a corporate fundraiser during its
annual corporate golf event. During the luncheon
which culminated the event, the president of the
company spoke about the cause. I was delighted to
hear him speak and he said that the company would
match whatever was collected that day. This was my
first introduction to good corporate stewardship as
companies and individuals dug deep into their pockets
and emptied out whatever was in their wallets.
Jamaican Dollars, US Dollars and checks were piled on
plates and we collected about $350,000 – my company
matched it and handed over $700,000.

As grateful as I was listening to the speech, there was
a part of it which hit me like a physical blow. As the

president spoke about why the company was doing this fundraiser he stated that one of their very own, Christine Staple-Ebanks, who had organized the event, had a 'handicapped' son As he spoke, every time he used the word 'handicapped' I recoiled and felt myself go kind of numb. I knew that this ignorance really deserved a response but it was hard to know what to say when the ignorance was personified in the head of my company, my boss, standing just inches away from me. So I just gave him a tight smile and said nothing. And of course I kicked myself for the rest of the day thinking of all the things I could have – should have – said. What bothered me most about his comments was the fact that I knew he meant well. I knew his heart was in the right place and I also knew that the words he used connected with the audience and contributed to their financial outpouring. Yet it was still painful. I shared the experience with Dawn that evening and her response was, "Sometimes the deepest word-wounds we experience come from well-intentioned persons." That comment has stayed with me to this day and has helped me to watch over the words that relate to my children, or any child for that matter.

Raising Nathan

While Nathan's new school had many limitations – underfunding, limited resources and inadequate facilities – for a brief while Nathan benefitted because as we were to discover he was a social butterfly in the making. Nathan worked his charm and had all the aunties, mommies, daddies and children at the school warming to him. He sought out the two prettiest girls, Rene and Gianni, who were both five or more years older than him, and established them as his girl-friends. They in turn were enamored and watched out for him.

But before long I became dissatisfied and disgruntled again. The truth was that while I didn't know what more I could do I knew that what I was seeing could not be all there was. So I resumed my research and need for answers.

As my workload picked up I was home less and less for Nathan's therapy. To compensate I developed a structured schedule for his day which included time working on his sitting, rolling, reaching and grasping, standing and playing. His caregiver was required to log his activities daily – his progress, his meals (how much and what he ate), and any signs that he may be coming down with something. This way I would at least have the records to check back on if I needed to do so. The system worked very well... or so I thought for a long while.

Raising Nathan

Chapter 22
The Unfolding Impact

Parents know that the birth of a child is life changing for the family. But this pales in comparison to the diagnosis of a disability. I do not mean to trivialize childbirth and parenting I am merely trying to draw a parallel so those who have (thankfully) never walked this path will have an idea of the magnitude of the change.

A long time ago my mother told me that when you become a parent you stop living for yourself and make decisions that are in the best interest of your child. This is all fine and well but when you have a child diagnosed with a major life-long disability what is in the best interest of the child becomes more paramount. In our case I believed that living in a country with very little social care and protection programmes, and limited intervention and special education for such persons with disabilities, that it was in our son's best interest for me to leave formal employment. Were it that we only had Nathan this may not have been seen as such a bad idea but having three other children, on the surface of it, quitting work seemed like a mistake.

Over the years I have tried many things to help Nathan including aquatherapy, hyperbaric oxygen therapy and conductive education. I've spent hundreds of hours researching alternative treatments, some way too invasive for me to try. I was, like most parents who get such a diagnosis, trying to find the cure. Then one day it hit me. After trying the umpteenth treatment for the umpteenth time and experiencing great disappointment when Nathan did not get up and walk, it dawned on me that my job was not to try and fix my son. My job was to love him like I do his siblings, care for him, nurture him, support him and give him the opportunity to develop, whatever that development may look like. In the same way that his older sister attends school and does karate as an extracurricular activity to develop her mind and body, or his brother Ryan plays football, goes out for track days and is a member of the cadets for his school, or his sister Jordanne does ballet – my job was not to cart Nathan around from therapy to therapy but rather to get him involved in activities that would develop his whole being. We enrolled Nathan in the school's extra curricular swimming programme and suffered the disappointment that similarly to all other things, we were forced to pay a premium because Nathan has 'special needs'.

Nevertheless, I do what I must because I know that if Nathan is to get the opportunities he needs to develop, I will have to play a role in creating these opportunities. Since his diagnosis I feel that my brain has not turned off even for one moment. My reading material has changed drastically and most of the books on my shelf at home are either Christian religion or disability/special education related. Making changes isn't easy – one cannot put a time frame on when change will come. But just because things get tough, I cannot afford to lose hope. My son and my family's future depend on me not giving up and sticking with it until I succeed.

In the beginning, nothing that I know now was ever just handed to me. It took me a long time to unravel the cerebral palsy disability and its effects. For that matter it took me months to say the words c-e-r-e-b-r-a-l p-a-l-s-y without tripping over my tongue! Now when I hear others trip over the pronunciation it helps me to realize just how intimate I have become with these two little words. I can readily recall that a year after the diagnosis neither Robert nor I were any closer to understanding what it was and what to do. Nathan remained hidden behind his condition because of his fragile state and all that loomed before me were his symptoms, his hospitalization, his surgery, his recovery and his developmental delays. During all those months I never thought of him as a baby, a child, a person who was in need of love, nurturing and silliness (goo goo ga ga)! All I saw was hospital, doctors, sterile environment, medicine and so on.

When we finally brought him home he was still very ill. He was fragile, limp and unconnected. There was no welcome home party, no visitors pouring in, there was just weariness and sadness most of the time. When he was diagnosed with cerebral palsy the weight of the diagnosis dragged us down and pushed him, the child, even further back. We didn't just buy him toys we bought him therapy toys, sensory aids, tactile aids – everything we did was so medicinal. The baby, the little baby that was still there was lost behind one crisis after another. His disability was foremost and then came the labels 'disabled child', 'CP baby' – my eyes from the very start saw only his deficit. Other people close to the family referred to him as the 'handicapped baby' or the 'deformed child'. Others still to this day refer to his condition as his 'sickness'. If I had a dollar for every time I have told someone that cerebral palsy is not a sickness, and see the pitying look in their eyes as if to say 'you are in denial', I would be rich today. But the impact of all these labels evoked deep shame in me and pity for my child, and for about two and a half years I lost sight of the child.

To this day I still come across people whose first question, "How is your son?" translates as, "Is he over his sickness?" Or those who when they find out I have a child with special needs immediately look embarrassed as they tell me how sorry they are. I have learned to respond, "Why are you sorry? I am not. We're not. He is not." In the beginning these were only words but as I got to know my son these words took on shape and life and meaning and became real.

Today I have a more informed response because I believe that Nathan and children like Nathan come into the world to teach us how to love unconditionally. They teach us about ourselves and build our faith. Children like Nathan teach us how fragile we are and at the same time how resilient and strong we are. I've watched Nathan and children who carry his special gift go through pain and struggles and I am always amazed at how mellow many of them are. While children with disabilities are children first, and exhibit the many peculiarities of budding personalities, I have found most of the children I have come to know over the years to be pleasant, easy to get along with and incredibly loving and caring. Many wear million dollar smiles that warm your heart to the core. When they have a problem you know right away for there is no pretending. They are not afraid to cry, to love, to hope or to care even in the midst of pain and challenging circumstances.

They treasure the little things in life: going for a walk outside is a big deal; going for a ride in the car is a major excursion; being held in an upright position, so that they can eat or watch TV is a great accomplishment. I have seen the way Nathan looked at a deer in a park in New Jersey once when we took him there for therapy and stayed with my sister Phyllis and her family. He epitomized the phrase 'wide-eyed wonder' as he stared at the animal, basking in its splendour. And in the next minute, when we helped him to feed the deer a piece of fruit and his hand was brushed by the animal's whiskers, he pulled his hand back waving it from side to side in a frantic gesture of 'no' which meant I don't like the feel of this thing on my hand so I would rather look and not touch.

In *The Wit and Wisdom of Mark Twain*, Twain says, "The difference between the right word and the almost right word is the difference between lightening and the lightening bug."[1]

An article that struck a chord with me when I was struggling to articulate how 'labels' were making me feel was 'People First Language' written by Kathy Snow. Snow – a wife and mother including having a child with disabilities, author, public speaker, trainer and consultant – states that words matter. She says that, "Old and inaccurate descriptors perpetrate negative stereotypes and generate an incredibly powerful and attitudinal barrier – the greatest obstacle facing individuals with disabilities." And, "That a disability is first and foremost only a medical diagnosis and that when we define people by their diagnosis, we devalue and disrespect them as individuals."[2] Well said Mrs Snow!

Many of our thought leaders today believe that the words we use to describe ourselves have an impact on our life. Contrary to the age-old 'sticks and stones may break my bones but words can never hurt me' lesson we learned as children, today we know for a fact that words do matter. For example, the creation story in the book of Genesis tells us that, *In the beginning... God said let there be light... and there was light.* (Genesis 1:3). All of creation came into being upon the spoken words of God. Man was the only act of creation where God used his hands to mould and shape man into His (God's) image and likeness. It is my view that as we are created in the image and likeness of God, that we have that same power to create with our words. We either build up, or tear down, block, or flow, enable or impede with our words.

The article continues, "For too long, people who happen to have conditions we call 'disabilities' have been subjected to devaluation, marginalization, prejudice and more."[2]

Growing up even talking about a disability or someone with a disability was taboo. There are families I have known all of my life and did not know that they had a child or family member with a disability. These individuals are hidden from life.

Snow also states, "The first way to devalue someone is through language, by using words or labels to identify a person/group as 'less-than' as 'the others – not like us' and so forth. Once a person/group has been identified this way, it makes it easier to justify prejudice and discrimination. Our language shapes our attitudes, our attitudes shape our language – they're intertwined. And our attitudes and language drive our actions!"[2]

Over the years, I have become passionate about using and promoting the use of People First Language. Why is this important? Because it is the right thing to do. Let me share an example of what I mean. Some years ago, I was at a forum organized by the Jamaica Council for Persons with Disabilities. It was well attended and my first revelation of the true number of persons – adults, children, parents, employees, business owners – with disabilities there were in Jamaica. Approximately 60 percent of the audience were themselves persons with disabilities. New organizations were invited to introduce their work and organization to the stakeholders. The founder of one of the new non-profits got up to speak.

Raising Nathan

Within moments of opening her mouth the labels began to fly, 'handicapped so and so', 'cripple people so and so'. With each label the buzz in the room grew louder and louder as persons took offence. Someone nudged the speaker and whispered something to her, she responded by saying, "Oh, I am sorry if I am using the wrong words, but I don't know what is the 'politically' correct term to use." I heard someone near to me mutter, "Well, you better sit down until you learn it." People took offense. I took offense because every label slapped me like a physical blow.

People First Language is not about political correctness, instead it demonstrates good manners, respecting the golden rule, 'do unto others, as you would do to yourself'. People First Language, "Can change the way we see a person, and it can change the way a person sees himself or herself!"[2]

I know that it did that for me. The day I made that shift in my head was the day everything changed. People First Language is important to me because it represents a more respectful, accurate way of communicating. My son is not his diagnosis or disability. He is a child first; his disability is merely an attribute of him, like brown eyes, black hair or glasses. When we take care to use People First Language we are saying to the person that we see them and not their disability. It took me a while to make this adjustment. When I did I became a true convert. Snow says, "Putting people first helps to eliminate old, prejudicial and hurtful descriptors."[2]

I agree wholeheartedly.

The United Nations Convention on the Rights of Persons with Disabilities (CRPD)[3] also supports the use of People First Language. This Convention is an international treaty led by the United Nations to protect persons with disabilities worldwide. The convention aims to change the light in which persons with disabilities are viewed to a more positive and diverse one. Specifically, countries that become party to the CRPD agree to promote, protect and ensure the full and equal enjoyment of all human rights and fundamental freedoms by all persons with disabilities and to promote respect for inherent dignity.

The general principles of the CRPD as articulated in Article 3 are:

(a) *Respect for inherent dignity, individual autonomy including the freedom to make one's own choices, and independence of persons;*

(b) *Non-discrimination;*

(c) *Full and effective participation and inclusion in society;*

(d) *Respect for difference and acceptance of persons with disabilities as part of human diversity and humanity;*

(e) *Equality of opportunity;*

(f) *Accessibility;*

(g) *Equality between men and women;*

(h) *Respect for the evolving capacities of children with disabilities and respect for the right of children with disabilities.*

The text for the CRPD was adopted by the United Nations General Assembly on 13 December 2006, and opened for signature on 30 March 2007. Jamaica was the first country in the world to sign and ratify the CRPD – the document was signed by the then Minister of State, Mr Floyd Morris who himself lives with the disability of blindness.

Diagnosed with glaucoma in high school, Floyd Morris had to come to terms with blindness at a young age. After being rehabilitated at the Jamaica Society for the Blind and educating himself to the highest level at the University of the West Indies, Floyd positioned himself to create change to impact the lives of others and helped to change the course of Jamaica and the world. In 1998, Floyd Morris became the first person with a major disability to be appointed to the Jamaican Senate and later to become a Minister of State. While still a Senator, Floyd used this powerful platform to drive policies and initiatives concerning persons with disabilities at many levels locally and internationally. His parliamentary contributions led to the approval of the National Policy on Disability and led to the creation of the Disability Bill, which was passed into law on 10 October 2014. Working in close collaboration with the community of persons with disabilities, some of his other accomplishments included getting the amendment to the Road Traffic Regulations in 2005 which paved the way for persons who are deaf to drive on Jamaican roads. Under his stewardship, the Margaret Moodie Scholarship was established to provide persons with disabilities scholarships to attend a tertiary institution of their choice. It was Senator Morris along with the late Mrs Faith Innerarity – veteran public servant, accomplished writer and scholar – who represented Jamaica in the historic negotiations, signing and ratification of the United Nations Convention on the Rights of Persons with Disabilities. There is a standing joke that so eager was Senator Morris for the CRPD to come into effect, that as the bearers were passing with the document, he signed it so fast that the ink was dry when the document touched down on the table. Senator Morris was bestowed the Prime Minister Award for Excellence in Disability Reform in 2012 for his stellar contribution to the development and welfare of persons with disabilities in Jamaica. In 2013, he was appointed President of The House of the Senate.

The Convention on the Rights of Persons with Disabilities has served as the major catalyst in the global movement from viewing persons with disabilities as objects of charity, medical treatment and social protection towards viewing them as full and equal members of society, with human rights. It is also the only UN human rights instrument with an explicit sustainable development dimension. The Convention was the first human rights treaty of the third millennium. As of April 2015, there are 159 signatories and 154 parties, including the European Union.

In spite of these developments I still hear people, even those who work with children and adults with disabilities, use references such as 'autistic', 'downs' kid, 'blind' man and 'crippled' man or woman, etc. One of the purposes of this book is to shine the spotlight on this very important issue. You see, the day I was finally to see beyond the label given my son... to see my child first, changed the way I saw him... and he was beautiful, as he is fearfully and wonderfully made.

We still have a long way to go to drive the message home.

Raising Nathan

Chapter 23

Cerebral Palsy is What I've Got,
Not Who I Am

It took me the most part of two years to meet my son. What do I mean by that? I'm glad you asked. As I had shared in previous chapters, in the early days following his birth, and everything leading up to his diagnosis and for the years following the diagnosis, it seemed that we moved from one crisis to another. Life was like a roller coaster ride with high highs and low lows, sharp twists and turns, and I was always off-balance as I struggled to hold on to the reins of my life. I believe I remained in crisis mode for the first two years of his life, and as such I had become very clinical about his process. This state, while essential for his well-being, robbed me of the opportunity to bond with my child. In all of my thoughts about him, by default, I went to his deficits and by the time I was done, there was no energy to look beyond. At two years old, I was still relatively new to the diagnosis, and while it is said 'ignorance is bliss', in my case it wasn't. Not knowing what I was up against was frightening, unsettling, fear-inducing and stressful. As a result of this state and the mindset I was in, every conversation about Nathan was about his disability. On one occasion, I was speaking with my friend Dawn when out of the blue she asked me, "What is Nathan's favourite colour?" This question threw me a curved ball, because it was quite unexpected. I grew silent to the point where she had to ask whether I was still on the phone. I sheepishly admitted that I didn't know what his favourite colour was. The truth was that I had never thought of it, because until that moment, I had never thought of Nathan the person.

Without skipping a beat, Dawn rolled off a series of follow up questions, "What was Nathan's favourite toy? What was his favourite food? What was his favourite thing to do with me, with his daddy, with his brother and sisters?" Tearfully I confessed that I didn't know. Without judgement and condemnation, Dawn simply asked, "Chrissy, have you met your son?" I was lost for words. She went on, "I want you to go home, sit with Mr Nathan and look into his eyes. The eyes are the windows to the soul. Go home and look into your son's eyes... go meet your son."

Cerebral Palsy is What I've Got, Not Who I Am

I was in my car and driving home at the time. When I arrived home it was afternoon and Nathan was perched in his usual position watching the television. I went up to him, turned off the television set, sat down and turned his wheelchair to face me. Usually interrupting him when he was watching the television was a no-no... turning off the television was tantamount to inflicting bodily harm upon him, and was usually met with sharp piercing screams which had everyone in the house running to his rescue. But this day, it was as if he sensed that we were about to experience something significant, because he did not resist me nor did he utter a word. I sat on eye level with him and cupped his little face in my hands to keep his head steady so I could look into his eyes. For the first time in his two and a half years, and the only time for that matter that I can remember, his head was steady and he held my gaze unflinchingly. As I gazed into his beautiful brown eyes, I noted how soft and warm they were. How the contrast of the whites of his eyes against the soft brown of his irises was striking. I noticed that he had inherited his paternal grandmother's blue ring at the base of his iris and around his pupils. I was reminded of his enviably long and plush black eyelashes. I melted into the sheer beauty, warmth and life in his eyes. I don't know how long our eyes were locked, but suddenly all else faded away and I saw my son for the very first time. I saw the light dancing in his eyes. I saw his joy, peace and wholesomeness. I saw the impish glint in his eyes, and suddenly I saw him. He was whole, there was nothing broken about him. I saw into his spirit and I felt life, energy and hope. I saw potential and purposefulness. I saw life! He started laughing and I joined in. We laughed and for the first time, I felt the joy of being his mother. In that moment I realized that I had met my child for the very first time. I didn't see his 'disability', I simply didn't care. Here was my child! Here was my son! My baby! My joy! And I whispered to him, "Hi sweetie pie, I am your mommy." He grinned from ear to ear. That was the day I met my son. He was two and a half years old.

My view of him shifted that day. It was as if a shroud was lifted, suddenly my vision was cleared. All of the stuff which had obscured my view of my child had disappeared, just like that! Shortly after that experience, my friend Wendean called me on the phone to share a thought she had about Nathan. She shared that it had entered into her spirit that since he was born, that we had been solely focussed on his issues, and that we had

never truly celebrated his birth. There were no birthday
parties, and none of the celebratory activities we had
done with our other children. She felt it was time we
threw a 'praise-party' to celebrate Nathan, that he
made it, and that he is a gift to us. I agreed. We planned
the party at her home, and less than one month later,
we had our first real celebration of the birth of our
child. The child was two and a half years old.

Those two experiences became the catalyst for the
change in my mindset about this 'gift from God', and
I also believe it began my healing. Within weeks, all
I could see was my beautiful little boy. I couldn't take
my eyes off him. I kept drinking deeply of all of him,
it was as if I was waking up from a slumber and making
up for the lost years. I also started researching other
articles about toddlers. As I did, I began to notice that
Nathan was achieving some of his developmental
milestones. When I started to look for his strengths, I
began to see them... there were more things that were
going right than what was 'wrong'! This was thrilling
beyond words. The more I freed myself to see him as a
person, the more I came to understand that there was
nothing to fear and that people with cerebral palsy
can go on to lead healthy and productive lives. In my

research I found out that there were many people with disabilities who have been contributing to society. I already spoke about Senator Morris and countless other Jamaicans. On the international stage, they are great actors, singers and other famous people. This excited me!

A few others who stood out for me included Dr. Janice Brunstrom, a pediatric neurologist specializing in cerebral palsy (CP) at St Louis Children's Hospital and Washington University. My research found that she is the only pediatric neurologist in the US who also has cerebral palsy, and she is one of the leading scientists in CP research. She started and leads the only comprehensive pediatric CP Centre in the country. Then there was Jerry Traylor, a motivational speaker with cerebral palsy. He was said, at the time, to be the only person to jog across the United States of America on crutches![1] My all time inspiration is Professor Stephen Hawking, author and scholar. Professor Hawking is the former Lucasian Professor of Mathematics at the University of Cambridge and author of the book *A Brief History of Time* which was an international bestseller. Now the Dennis Stanton Avery and Sally Tsui Wong-Avery Director of Research at the

Department of Applied Mathematics and Theoretical Physics and Founder of the Centre for Theoretical Cosmology at Cambridge. His other books for the general reader include *A Briefer History of Time*, the essay collection *Black Holes and Baby Universe* and *The Universe in a Nutshell*. In 1963, Professor Hawking contracted motor neurone disease and was given two years to live. Yet he went on to Cambridge to become a brilliant researcher and Professorial Fellow at Gonville and Caius College. Professor Hawking has over a dozen honorary degrees and was awarded the **Commander** *of the Most Excellent Order of the British Empire* (**CBE**) in 1982. He is a fellow of the Royal Society and a Member of the US National Academy of Science, and is regarded as one of the most brilliant theoretical physicists since Einstein. My son is in very good company! I have come to realize that my child could become who he came here to be, and the only limitations he faced were those put on him by those around him – me, his father, family, school and his external environment.[2]

This revelation opened up my interest in finding out everything I could to grow my knowledge and build my capacity.

Simply put, cerebral palsy is a neurological non-progressive disorder that permanently affects movement and muscle coordination. It is caused by damage to the motor control centres of the developing brain mostly from pregnancy but also during childbirth and after birth up to about three years of age.[3]

There are four main causes of brain damage. The first is damage that looks like tiny holes in the white matter (tissue) of the brain. White matter is responsible for transmitting signals both inside the brain and to the rest of the body – any gaps in the brain tissue interferes with the normal transmission of signals. Researchers have posited that the period of selective vulnerability in a developing fetal brain in which periventricular white matter is particularly sensitive to insults and injury is between 26 and 34 weeks.[4] Neither the CT scan nor the MRI identified this as the cause of Nathan's cerebral palsy so it was ruled out by the neurologist.

The second cause of damage is abnormal development of the brain. Mutations in the genes that control fetal brain development can stop the brain from developing normally or any interruption of the normal process of brain growth can cause brain malformations that interfere with the transmission of brain signals. Infections, fevers, trauma or other factors that cause unhealthy conditions in the womb also put an unborn baby's nervous system at risk.[4] These were also ruled out in Nathan's case.

The third cause is bleeding in the brain. Bleeding inside the brain from blocked or broken blood vessels is commonly caused by a fetal stroke. Babies can suffer a stroke while still in the womb because blood clots in the placenta block the flow of blood in the brain. Other types of fetal stroke are caused by malformed or weak blood vessels in the brain or by blood-clotting abnormalities. Maternal high blood pressure (hypertension) is a common medical disorder during pregnancy and can be a cause of babies having a stroke. Maternal infections, especially pelvic inflammatory disease, have also been shown to increase the risk of fetal strokes.[4] I did not suffer from hypertension during the pregnancy and bleeding in the brain was ruled out.

The fourth cause of brain damage stems from a severe lack of oxygen. Asphyxia, a lack of oxygen in the brain caused by an interruption in breathing or poor oxygen supply, is common for a brief period of time in babies due to the stress of labour and delivery. If the supply of oxygen is cut off or reduced for lengthy periods, a baby can develop a type of brain damage called hypoxic-ischemic encephalopathy which destroys tissue in the cerebral motor cortex and other areas of the brain. This kind of damage can also be caused by severe maternal low blood pressure; rupture of the uterus; detachment of the placenta; problems involving the umbilical cord; or severe trauma to the head during labour and delivery.[4]

We knew that Nathan's left lung had not developed properly. My OB/GYN's instruction from the moment Nathan was born was to put him in an incubator before cutting his umbilical cord. But this was not done and there was a period of time before he was taken to the NICU and put on assisted breathing when he could have lacked oxygen. There were also other moments – several times during the early days that Nathan's ventilator malfunctioned and the machine would trigger a loud beeping and all the lights would go haywire. A nurse would rush in to us and at times I would be asked to leave the room. At other times I was forgotten as the nurse would come and adjust the equipment and it would go back to its steady beeping.

We do not know for sure exactly when the damage was done, but Nathan developing severe jaundice during the night of his tenth day, and it only being brought into control on the 11th day, gave us a window when we believe that it happened.

Once the damage is done, it is done. People have asked me whether cerebral palsy is an infectious disease. Nathan's first caregiver told me that her boyfriend said if they were to be together she had to give up her job of working with the 'disabled' baby, as should they have a child together he didn't want their child to be infected. She showed him the highway... good for her! Cerebral palsy is not an infectious disease and it is not contagious.

The look and presentation of cerebral palsy can be off putting. The condition is often characterized by abnormal muscle tone, reflexes, or motor development and coordination. There can be joints and bone deformities and contractures (permanently fixed tight muscles and joints). The classical symptoms are spasticity, spasms, other involuntary movements (e.g. facial gestures), unsteady gait, problems with balance, and/or soft tissue findings consisting largely of decreased muscle mass. Scissor walking (where the knees come in and cross) and toe walking (which can contribute to a gait reminiscent of a puppet) are common among people with CP who are able to walk. On the whole, CP symptoms are diverse.[5]

Speech and language disorders are common in people with cerebral palsy. An estimated 31–88 percent of children with cerebral palsy are reported to have problems associated with speech, poor respiratory control and oral articulation disorders that are due to restricted movement in the oral-facial muscles. Children with cerebral palsy are at risk of learned helplessness and becoming passive communicators, initiating little communication.[5]

These are but a few of the reasons that early stimulation, intervention and parent education must become a crucial management strategy. They are also the reasons that individuals with cerebral palsy often require a lifetime of care and support. People with cerebral palsy are not helpless but need help getting some things done. This requires carefully planning the life of a child to ensure that they are given the support they need to develop holistically. There are currently no known cures for cerebral palsy. Management, including efforts to treat and prevent complications, is critical.

The years preceding my own enlightenment were characterized by bouts of sickness – frequent fevers, colds and respiratory tract infections. In my learning, I also became quite skilled at administering first aid, whether it was applying a hand pump or a nebulizer machine. I learned how to spot the first signs of a cold and how to apply chest therapy to break up colds. Nathan's life and health depended on me being a quick learner.

Through Nathan, I have come to meet some great people in Jamaica with cerebral palsy. One such person is Rene Lambert. She attended Nathan's first formal school and his present school. There was an instant attraction of her to Nathan and him to her. And while I know she considered him a cute kid and little brother, he was in love with her. He was three and she was about seven, he flirted with her outrageously. It was the cutest thing to watch. Rene has cerebral palsy but refuses to let it keep her back. She has sass, spunk and is brilliant. She wrote the poem, *I am Beautiful and Bold* which says:

Raising Nathan

Cerebral palsy is what I've got, C.P. is what I'm not.

It restricts me from living my life how I want,
but I will not be bound.

I'm beautiful and bold.

I adopted this poem as a kind of theme for my son and for all the children out there who are told that they can 'never, never, never'. I was liberated from the limitations imposed by his diagnosis!

Chapter 24

The Impact of the 'Disability' on the Family

I continued with my research, but this time from an empowered vantage point. I now understood that *knowledge is power*, and the right knowledge would help me to help my child.

What do I mean by the 'impact of the disability on the family'? All parents know that parenting typically developing children is challenging. Parents of a child with disabilities know that the implications of caring for their child with a disability are considerable. Modesta Pousada attributes this to the fact that, "Parents have to cope with many changing demands related to the specific needs of their child."[1] Within Nathan's first two years I realized that I was faced with two options. Option one would be to continue in formal employment and keep Nathan in a maintenance mode, a day-care situation where his health and well-being were looked after. Or option two, was for me to be at home and drive his development through research and building up the services that he and other children like him would need. I am glad that I have a husband who saw the big picture from the start. Though giving up my job, a steady income and my independence was significant, he agreed with me that the latter option was what his heart felt that we needed to do in order to better support our son.

Research informs that the costs associated with raising a child with cerebral palsy are usually greater than those of an adult with cerebral palsy. This is because the needs of a growing child tend to vary and change more quickly than those of an adult. In our case, Nathan came into the world at a high cost. His stay in hospital ran just under a half a million – thank goodness for health insurance. Due to his frequent bouts of illness, medication was needed right away and within six months of Nathan coming home we were out of funds. The burden of care fell fully into our laps due to the lack of available social services. So we adjusted the only way we knew how, by cutting back on non-essentials and living from pay cheque to pay cheque.

My marketing and event planning job took me away from home a lot and for the first year and a half after my return to work I travelled frequently for a two to three day stretch at a time, organizing and overseeing corporate events for my company. After months of this schedule I started longing to see my children in daylight so I flew in from Montego Bay early one day and went directly home from the airport. It was about 5pm when I arrived and I saw that Nathan was asleep. I thought it a bit odd as he had long left daytime naps behind. He was two-and-a-half years old and in some ways had adopted the habits of a toddler, so napping in the afternoon was very unusual for him.

I asked his caregiver how he had come to be asleep and she said he'd had a very active day and that he seemed to be coming down with a cold. Disappointed that I couldn't spend time with him, I let him be. The next morning I had an early morning meeting and Nathan was still asleep and appeared drowsy when I tried to rouse him. I left resolving to return home earlier that afternoon so I could see him. When I arrived home at 3:30pm that afternoon I saw that Nathan was asleep again. His caregiver was gone and the housekeeper told me that she had some sort of emergency and so had left early. This concerned me greatly. I checked Nathan's log book and saw that the caregiver had not recorded much for that day. I then took the opportunity to check through the book for the week before and saw that all the entries stated the same information. I checked back two weeks, three weeks and saw that all of the entries across a span of four weeks contained the same information. I dug out all of the older log books and could not believe my eyes when I saw that the exact same information was recorded in all of them, going back six months. It was then that I realized that it looked like the care-giver had not been carrying out any of the activities and tasks as assigned.

Each week, Nathan's therapist would come to visit and leave behind a set of early stimulation activities for the caregiver to carry out with him at set times during the day. Early stimulation is a set of techniques, and science-based activities which are applied systematically and sequentially, the goal of which is to recognize and encourage the potential of each individual child and present challenges and appropriate activities to strengthen and optimize their cognitive, physical, emotional and social development. Simply put, these activities were not optional, but critical to Nathan's development and long term outcomes. Learning that his caregiver might not be carrying out these activities was devastating. But as I wasn't sure, I kept what I had discovered between Robert and myself until I could learn more.

The next day was Friday. Nathan had not yet awakened and I was determined to get to the bottom of what was going on. I roused him and saw that his little face was flushed red, his eyes were weak looking and his smile was not at its usual brilliance. He now had a fully blown fever. I toyed with whether I should go out of town to Montego Bay as planned, or take him to the doctor. As I thought about what I should do, Adrianne came downstairs and told me that she had had a bad dream. She dreamt that there was a large python (snake) in our house and that it slithered upstairs and went into the boys' bedroom. I am not generally a superstitious person but that settled my decision, I would take Nathan to the doctor. I called my assistant and asked her to change my flight from 10am to 2:15pm. I dressed Nathan and we headed to his pediatrician – thankfully we were seen almost right away. Nathan's doctor, Dr Andrea Dewdney, was present and I was glad. She was intimately familiar with his history and I often refer to her as his 'wife', a nickname she wears happily.

Raising Nathan

As I walked into the room she asked, "What's wrong with my pumpkin now?" She took one look at him and before I could even sit down said, "Mrs Ebanks, I don't like how Nathan is looking. I know it is flu season, so I am going to order a chest X-ray." I took the referral note and went downstairs to the lab. Less than 30 minutes later we were back in her office. She looked at the lab report and without lifting her eyes asked, "Where is Nathan's daddy?" I told her he was at work. "Ask him to pack a bag for Nathan and meet you at University Hospital, it is worse that I suspected. Nathan has a bad case of pneumonia; his left lung is on the verge of collapsing. We need to get him to the hospital right away and admit him, he is very sick." Ten minutes later with the referral and X-ray in hand, I was racing in my car towards the hospital which was less than ten minutes away.

We arrived at the hospital and encountered our first hurdle as there were no parking spaces anywhere near the emergency room. I circled the car park a few times before signaling to the security guard. Luckily after I explained that my child was really sick, the guard allowed me to park in an unmarked area so I could get Nathan inside. Shortly after we got there, Robert's parents' arrived. I was glad for the company.

The admission process was surprisingly long and tedious. We had arrived at the hospital at about 11:30am and presented the referral at the front desk. I was told to sit until I heard my son's name. It was about 30 minutes later that his name was called. We were sent into another room and given a number. We had to sit on a bench for almost an hour before his number was finally called. This was the second point in the registration process. We sat with a nurse who took all of my history from my first pregnancy through to Nathan. It took a long time. When she was done, we were sent back to the bench to wait. Nearly another hour later Nathan was finally called in to see the doctor. She was a young resident who went through his entire case history again, in excruciating detail. She slowed down even more when I told her that he was born at the hospital, all of our records were there and that I had already given all of these details to the nurse outside. She told me that this was the process and the faster I answered the questions the quicker we could move forward so I dutifully answered her questions. It was now after 2pm and no one had taken a look at Nathan. He was invisible.

Finally the doctor was finished with us and I was asked to sit back outside and wait. Another nurse who was busying around when I got there kept looking at Nathan and asked if we were heading over to the ward. I told her that the doctor said we were to sit back outside. She was not happy and remarked, "Don't they see that this baby is very sick." She knocked on the consultation room door and went inside. After a few minutes she came back with a chart in her hand and told me to follow her – she was taking us to the ward. I was grateful for her intervention.

Nathan was admitted on the children's ward which was downstairs and in the building across from the NICU where he had been a critical patient for the first 24 days of his life. The place did not hold good memories for me and I had tried to scrub the experience from my mind. This was the first time I'd seen the building since Nathan's discharge more than two years before. That day I could have well done without the reminder that he almost didn't make it.

We got to the ward and I was put on another bench to sit just outside the large dormitory style ward. It was now about 3:30pm. After a while, yet another nurse came to me with a file and began to ask me the same questions I had answered when we had first arrived, when we had registered, before we saw the doctor, and in great detail with the doctor. At that point I simply lost it. I told her in my most authoritative voice that his files were at the hospital and I had spent the whole morning and into the afternoon answering the same questions over and over again and that I would not answer another question until someone put him in a bed and gave him something for the fever as he was burning up and had not taken any food or drink all day.

The new nurse was taken aback but when the other nurse told her we had been there since 11:30am, she settled Nathan in a bed, set up an intravenous drip and gave him some medicine for the fever through the drip. I sat by his bedside while she was doing all this. When she was done she picked up the clipboard again and said, "Now back to the questions." I sighed but obliged and answered the questions. My intended trip out of town was long forgotten.

Raising Nathan

Nathan's stay on the ward was very eventful. He was forgotten for most of the meal times and the one time they actually remembered him, they brought him soup with dumplings – it was recorded in all of the notes taken that he was still on pureed food and could not tolerate food with rough textures. We resorted to bringing him meals from home. We organized a twenty-four hour shift around him – I did the morning shift, our housekeeper did the afternoon shift and Robert did the night shift.

On one of the days when I was in the hospital's kitchen preparing a bottle of formula for Nathan, a nurse entered the room and asked who I was. I told her my son was a patient. She told me that I was in a restricted area which was only open to hospital staff. I told her that as they were not feeding my son I had no choice but to do so myself. She looked at me and then left me alone. For the four and a half days that Nathan was in hospital no one bothered me again when I was in the kitchen. No one brought him food either.

The second night that Nathan was at the hospital and I was waiting for Robert to arrive, I noticed a little girl in the bed across the room from Nathan's. It was an open ward with a number of beds and every one had a child in it. She was about seven years old, dark skinned and slim built. She was in bed groaning and wailing loudly and no one was paying her any attention. (This is one of the reasons I hate hospitals, I cannot bear to see people – particularly children – in distress and being ignored). As I sat with Nathan it reaffirmed for me why we would not leave him by himself, while he was there. My heart went out to the little girl who I learned had sickle cell. From the bits and pieces I gathered from other parents, she lived with her grandfather in rural Jamaica and her mother was away in the United States. She had stayed out in the rain weeks before and had caught a bad cold which was left unchecked. She developed an infection but apparently her family waited too long to bring her to the hospital. I had never witnessed death before but as I watched her aunt who was trying to feed her a meal I knew she was dying. Her eyes were rolling backwards into her head and she was not responding to her aunt's coaxing. Her head was rolling from side to side as her poor aunt tried to get her to eat from a plate she was holding. I felt a deep sadness for her and I silently prayed for her.

Raising Nathan

Robert came and I left. The next morning when I arrived for my shift I found him outside. He said that one of the children had gone into crisis a short while before and an emergency team had rushed in and ushered all visitors out. I knew even without asking that it was the little girl. He was visibly shaken as he told me that he had been watching and praying for her all night because he felt she was dying. He said she kept groaning and wailing throughout the night and no one went to her. At one point she was crying for the nurse and he said when he could not take it any longer he went to the nurse's station and asked if they did not hear the little girl crying for help. One of the nurses replied, "It is medication she wants, but we can't give her no more." He said around midnight the sound of her crying changed and he wanted to help her, but felt helpless. At about 6am she went into crisis and that was when a medical team rushed in. She didn't make it. The team was still there doing the post-clean up. I wept. I could see that Robert had been crying too.

I vowed that this would be Nathan's last bout with the hospital. Two days later he was discharged. As we drove with him out of the hospital compound I prayed and asked the Lord to let this be the last crisis which required admission to this hospital. God granted us that wish – Nathan has celebrated his 11th birthday recently and has never been back to the University Hospital of the West Indies.

Raising Nathan

Chapter 25

The Roller Coaster of Cerebral Palsy on Daily Life

It is true that the roller coaster effect of dealing with the many ups and downs of cerebral palsy can be emotionally exhausting and may leave little time or patience for parents to deal with any other children in the household. This was certainly the case in our household. Nathan's care swallowed up most of our evenings and weekends, and after a while became a huge challenge. Even after quitting my job I still found it to be difficult, as we now needed to balance the social and school lives of his siblings, which included a vortex of birthday parties, social gatherings and extra lessons. It took deliberateness and commitment to set aside time for his siblings so that their needs could also be addressed. But it would be years before I could take time out for me; for my needs to be addressed – without feeling guilty.

Raising Nathan

The challenges of daily life which we encountered fell into areas:

Communication: My life was on the go all of the time. Couple moments were few and far between – when Robert and I were not at work, we each took turns sleeping while the other worked around the house. Our lives were quite interesting. We had four children ranging from zero to eight. As if our hands were not full enough, we also hosted one of our friends' daughters who was seven. Our friend Rosie (Rose-Marie who was also my shared assistant at work) was pregnant with her second child. Rosie was having a difficult pregnancy with multiple hospitalizations, so to assist and support her, we kept her daughter Shanice, who was at the same school and in the same grade as our son Ryan. Shanice lived with us Sundays to Fridays for almost four months. So we now had five children between the ages of zero and eight. Truth be told, I enjoyed the challenge. It was great having another child in the household. I saw the stares when I went grocery shopping with all of them in toe. Once I was in the supermarket when a Rastafarian (dreadlocks as we call them in Jamaica) came up to me to hail me. He walked up to me, looked at the children and back to me and said, "Well done dawta." Rastafarians in Jamaica were known at the time to have many children... or 'have out their lot'. And so being told that I had done well by one of them... I wasn't sure how to take that.

The down side of having a house full of children was that we were kept busy. For those early months and years we lived in a state of 'survival mode'. Communicating normally was a challenge. Communicating with Nathan was a significant challenge. How do you communicate with a child who has no speech?

Early literacy: I shared earlier how I learned that Nathan was a child before his disability. As such, he was entitled to an education just like his siblings. This lesson was most vivid when he was two years old and I met Yvonne.

Yvonne was a mother of two boys, both of whom had special needs. One of her sons had attention deficit disorder (ADHD). And the second child had a condition called velocardiofacial syndrome (VCFS), a genetic condition that is sometimes hereditary, and is characterized by a combination of medical problems that vary from child to child. These medical problems include: heart defects; learning problems; speech; eye problems; feeding problems which include food coming through the nose (nasal regurgitation) because of the palatal differences; middle-ear infections (otitis media); low calcium due to hypoparathyroidism (low levels of the parathyroid hormone that can result in seizures); immune system problems which make it difficult for the body to fight infections; differences in the way the kidneys are formed or how they work; weak muscles; differences in the spine such as curvature of the spine (scoliosis) or bony abnormalities in the neck or upper back; and tapered fingers.[1]

Yvonne shared that her son had about 104 symptoms. She shared her journey and how she had to quit her job to sit outside of his learning institution so the boy would not run away from class. She told us that one day, it was like someone switched on a light and just like that, her son's brain fired up to the point that his teachers could not keep up with him. It seemed that he was a maths genius. She tried to enter him for the Caribbean Secondary School Examination (CXC) for maths, but the deadline for registering for the exam had passed. She went to the examination office and did not stop until they accepted his registration for the maths exam. Her son was about 17 at the time and as I listened to her I was deeply inspired.

She broke her account of her story to ask where Nathan attended school. I told her that he was not yet in school as he was barely two years old, and that I wanted to 'fix' his body first. She stared straight into my eyes, and repeated the question. Thinking she had not heard me the first time, I repeated my response. Still staring into my face she asked the question a third time. I gave her a variation of my answers and she repeated the question yet again. I got the message. She then shared that it is very important for every child with or without a disability to attend school. It was their inalienable human right and it was our only response as adults, to create the opportunities for all children to get quality and equitable education. I took it as a cue that she was 'gently suggesting' that I paid attention to my son's cognitive development. This was affirmed, when I later learned that this was one of the fundamental rights of every child under the Declaration of Human Rights and the Right of the Child conventions; and the United Nations Convention of Rights for Persons with Disabilities (UNCRPD). I was denying my child his fundamental human rights and compromising his development. We met on the Thursday and by the following Monday I had started a search for an early childhood learning institution for my child. Within two months I had him enrolled.

Mobility: Cerebral palsy is often called a 'movement disorder'. Many children with CP experience difficulty moving around in their environment. This can range from problems turning over in bed, to not being able to move on the floor, or difficulties with walking. Often the children may need more time or need to use a walking aid or wheelchair. These required the built environment – home, school, public roadways and public buildings to be accessible. In Nathan's case, his movement difficulty affected his whole body. His earlier floppiness had scaled up to fluctuating tones. He would go from being stiff one minute to being floppy the next. This affected seating equipment and wheel-chairs as he would slide around in the chair if it had too much space. We also worked to get him to roll and crawl commando style on the floor to get around. But this did not amount to much as he was not interested in lying on his belly, and when he did, he was in a hurry to get off of it. Also, his left side seemed to be most affected and his hand and leg on the left side would get stuck when he tried to move and we would have to help him release them. Therapy did help somewhat but it has not been consistent enough to deliver the desired effect.

Accessibility: Accessibility is another major challenge. By accessibility here, I am referring to the ease of getting into buildings. Moving a vehicle to enable or give people with disabilities 'ability to access' and benefit from some system or entity.[1] In our case, this meant physical access to the built environment – school, home, public buildings such as stores, movie theatre, church etc. This was a great challenge for us as very few buildings in Jamaica are accessible. We went to one tourist attraction once and were happy to see a ramp leading to the ticket booth, but were also appalled as that was where the access ended. We had to lift his wheelchair (a very heavy wheelchair) down what felt like hundreds of steps to take him into the facility and when we got there, found there was no place to put the chair. The concept of accessible design also focuses on enabling access to education and learning for children with disabilities through the use of special education and assistive technology. This particular challenge was the genesis for the formation of the Nathan Ebanks Foundation, a non profit organization which we formed when Nathan turned three, to support the inclusion, participation and empowerment of children with disabilities and their families, but that is the topic of another story.

Mealtimes: Mealtimes were particularly stressful for our family as Nathan always had to be held upright by someone and fed, which was a very slow and messy process. Not having an adaptive highchair which would help him to stay seated in an upright position meant that he had to sit in his stroller to be fed. At the end of the meal the majority of the food and drink were all over the floor, over him, over his clothes and over the chair – not much of the food was eaten. It was a draining experience for all of us, compounded by our worries about him choking and throwing up, which he seemed to do a lot.

Personal care: Washing, bathing and dressing were also great challenges. Often parents say that there is just not enough time especially if the child needs more assistance or uses specialized equipment for the bath and toilet. Nathan needed all of this equipment, and with the exception of a bath chair which we had bought, we had to work with him without these. This deeply impacted our family, and our ability to 'get going' for any occasion. As a result, we did not attend many social activities, and when we did go out, we were mostly late.

Medical and therapy appointments: It is fair to say that a child with a disability such as cerebral palsy will have more appointments than most – in the beginning it felt like we had a permanent seat at the doctors' and specialist's offices. You know when you have been somewhere too often, when all of the workers know you by your first name. Though I wasn't yet to realize it, the doctors' visits became less frequent as Nathan got older.

Balance: I took on the role of being Nathan's caregiver after he came home from hospital. As he grew and his care needs expanded I took on those roles too. In addition to the caring activities, I also carried out his exercise and therapy activities which were continuous from the moment he woke up in the morning, until he went to bed at night. And I became his teacher as well. These activities consumed me from sun-up until sun-down, seven days a week. Before long I was drained and experiencing burnout. I had no energy for my other children or my husband. I was tired all of the time, cranky and very unhappy.

A parent I met gave me a very valuable insight. She told me that I had to choose whether I was going to be my son's mother or his caregiver. She said it was two distinct roles. If I was his caregiver, I would be too tired to be his mom. However, if I hired someone to be his care giver, then my hands and heart would be free to love him. It proved to be the best advice I've ever received from another mom.

When Nathan was two years old, I discussed it with my husband and though we could not see how we could afford a nanny, we decided to take a step of faith and hire one anyway. The day we found and hired a nanny was one of the best days of my life since Nathan came home from the hospital. It came at a great sacrifice but it was worth it, because giving the care-giving role to another freed me to play with my child, to love him, to just be his mom. It was liberating and we have never looked back. It is amazing how you can find a way to do what you need to do. Not that it is easy having a full time caregiver in our employ, but this didn't just take the strain off me but off our whole family. An added bonus was that I didn't have to contend with being the bad guy when he didn't want to do his exercises or take a dose of nasty tasting medicine. The biggest result of this decision was the development and strengthening of the parent-child bond which surprisingly, I didn't even know was not there, until it was there. Over the years I have seen many parents of children, young and older, with disabilities who are worn out and have never, even for one day, enjoyed a proper parent and child relationship.

Raising Nathan

Chapter 26

I Didn't Think It Would Be This Hard

The day I resigned from my job to stay home and look after Nathan was another bittersweet day. We had thought long and hard before coming to the decision – and I had thought that when you make this type of decision, the road ahead would be easier. I had thought that the joy of being able to be there for Nathan and his siblings, who were still young children, would have been enough to help me ride the loss. But it wasn't.

I felt like a ship without a sail. It was as if I was in the middle of a vast ocean and I had lost my way. I was more confused than ever. It is one thing not to know as one cannot be held accountable for what one doesn't know. But once I began to gather information and become aware of Nathan's disability I felt more educated. On one hand, I felt that I had made the right decision to quit my job, but once it was done I was inflamed with guilt and regret. I was fearful to share the news with other family members because I felt they would not understand, and perhaps rightly so. It made little sense that I would choose to quit my job at a time when we needed money the most.

I now knew that Nathan was in need of early intervention and therapeutic stimulation. But I could find no local organization that offered this service. I didn't become aware of two state run intervention services – *Early Stimulation/Stimulation Plus* and *Rural Services for Children with Disabilities* – until Nathan was about two years old. Even if I had learned about the services earlier it would not have mattered because both services were oversubscribed with long waiting lists. I was disappointed nonetheless that the post surgery clinic at UHWI didn't seem to know about these programmes – they were the best kept secrets from those who needed to know. Up until that point and for another five years to come the full burden of care – comprehensive assessments and intervention, specialized equipment, and special education, was borne by my immediate family: my husband and me; my husband's parents; my mom; and one of my sisters.

My heartache was compounded when I noticed the phone had stopped ringing. Because of my job my mobile phone would ring non stop. I had to turn it off in the evenings when I was leaving work to get a breather. My children complained that mommy was always on the phone. I was that parent driving them to or from school that would arrive on the phone, drive them home still on the phone, drop them off and give instructions to the housekeeper while still on the phone, and leave still on the phone! The day I left my job the phone went silent. There was one time when I ran into someone from my former professional circle who jokingly said they did not recognize me because I didn't have a phone glued to my ear. I did not find the comment funny because the truth was I did not recognize myself either.

Within a month of leaving my job the decision became real in many ways but the financial reality was the most brutal. It wasn't long before I received the first of what became many calls from Credit Union – the loan on the cars was past its due date and there was no money to pay them. I could not say I will make the payment on the 25th because there was no money coming in. From then onwards it was like a sinking fund. Robert's salary would get swallowed up as soon as he was paid, with a multitude of bills remaining.

Raising Nathan

We continued to chop our budget and leisure activities were the first to go. We did not go to the movies together as a family for another five years.

Vacations went as well. We made our last trip to our favourite family resort in Runaway Bay on Jamaica's north coast in 2006, a venue that had been our annual family getaway since Adrianne was born in 1996. It had been a time of year to which I looked forward. The resort had a nanny service and so, for one glorious weekend each year, the children were entertained by a trained nanny and Robert and I got to sleep. The staff had come to know us and that last year when we went to the beach bar the waiter told us that he had just seen our kids and how much they had grown. It was my one place to completely refresh myself.

Then our clothing budget went. For the next five years my children learned to wear hand-me-downs and hand-me-ups from each other and from cousins, because there was no money for new clothes or shoes. I struggled with this and with not being able to just go out and buy an item of clothing because my children had outgrown what they had. The flow of money had diminished and so we had to make informed decisions while spending our available funds on loan reductions and school fees. We also took the children out of their school and for a while had a friend tutor them instead, as we could no longer afford to send them to a private school and I didn't think they would survive a public school.

Little by little all of the small pleasures went such as renting a movie, buying ice cream at Devon House, buying fast food – our lives had dwindled down to a hand to mouth existence. This was too tough for me to bear so I made myself busy. But I couldn't shake the feeling that I had fallen and couldn't get up.

Six months after leaving my job my pension contribution came in. I used the money to pay off the smaller loans, lower some of the other loans and clear the arrears for the cars. We put both cars on the market shortly after that and sadly when a buyer came it was for the minivan, the vehicle that we really needed, but we had to sell it so we could clear the remainder of the loan on the second vehicle.

I was miserable, deeply depressed and feeling crushed. How could I have made such a selfless decision and yet feel such hurt? We decided to give up our house and move in with Robert's parents. They had the space and it would also mean that a family member would always be around Nathan – I was not going to put him in a position where he could be taken advantage of again. I still believe to this day that if his caregiver had done what she was being paid to do, Nathan would have been further along developmentally.

Chapter 27

Thrown a Lifeline

One of the most significant contributions on this journey was from my friendship with Dawn as she helped me to see my son. Dawn entered my life during the last year of my job – she was the supervisor in the company's call centre and had a bubbly personality. Dawn had already been working two floors below me from before I joined the organization but we hadn't met. She came into the building after me in the mornings and left after me – and I did not have reason to visit the call centre much and so did not know she existed.

Early in my pregnancy with Nathan I was one of the lead coordinators for a technology expo. I had inherited the event and saw that my predecessor usually drew staff for the expo from other departments in our organization, particularly the call centre. I sent out a company-wide email seeking volunteers and Dawn replied. We spoke on the phone and I was immediately drawn to her. She was humorous with a light 'Tinkerbell' kind of laughter that was deeply infectious. I selected her before we'd even met and wrote to request her participation for the three days of the event. Dawn's supervisor called me almost as soon as I hit send on the email to ask if I had met Dawn and was I sure that I wanted her as part of my team. When I did finally meet Dawn I saw why he had asked – she was 545lbs. But that did not matter to me at all. Though she was never aware of this I fought for her to be part of my event team and won.

I finally met Dawn on the opening day of the expo. I had put a structure in place so someone else was responsible for organizing the floor team. After the opening ceremony the doors of the expo were opened and a flood of people came in. I had been working for 48 hours straight and had stepped into the event secretariat to catch my breath when I heard this voice saying, "Mrs Ebanks, I fixed this plate for you, come sit here and get something to eat." I looked up from the clipboard I was holding and saw this beautiful woman in African print. I liked her immediately. I thanked her and was about to take the plate and drink she was offering when I received a call that I was needed to escort some VIP guests around. I left immediately.

On three occasions that day every time I stepped back into the room there was Dawn offering me something to eat. And each time I could not take up the offer because I was called away before I had a chance! Finally at about 3pm I went to collect some giveaways from the secretariat to replenish the stock in the company's booth. This time Dawn's tone was firm, "I have been watching you all day and you have not even had a sip of water. I want you to sit here beside me now and eat this or I will hold you down and feed you myself!" She was serious. I sat down and ate some of the meal before flying away again. The memory stuck with me. In the two years I spent coordinating the company's functions no one else ever expressed a care for whether or not I ate.

I did not see her again for what seemed like ages because our paths never crossed. We spoke on the phone once in a while and then seven months into my pregnancy when I was sent home to rest, Dawn phoned. She was so easy to talk to and a great listener. She knew the right questions to ask to get me to share my problems and before I knew it we were on the phone for hours. Dawn would encourage me with Scriptures from the Bible and curiously relevant and timely anecdotes, and she always had a unique view of things. She called me daily from then onwards which helped to keep me sane during my two months of bed rest. Dawn later told me that I had made a good impression on her because I was one of the few people who never batted an eyelid when I finally met her.

The day Nathan was born I was lying in bed in the hospital at about 6pm when I opened my eyes to find Dawn sitting at my bedside. I knew it was a sacrifice for her because getting to the ward meant a long walk up several flights of stairs. In the gloomy and much too-public hospital room Dawn was a pleasant sight for sore eyes. Before long she had me laughing so hard that I was afraid we would both get kicked out of the ward! Luckily it was visiting hours so the nurses were lenient.

For the next four years Dawn became a lifeline for me. She always seemed to know when I was sinking into one of those dark pits because the phone would ring and it would be her calling. At first I did not always want to speak to her and I am sure she could hear me whispering frantically to Robert or one of my children, "Tell her I am sleeping," or "Tell her I can't come to the phone." She would always reply, "Tell Chrissy I am just calling to say that I love her and that I am praying for her. And I will call back." Without ceasing she did. Her persistence wore me down and little by little I accepted her calls. Before long I would look forward to her calls. And the next thing I knew I began to initiate the calls.

Dawn was a faithful friend. She was a great listener and had such a loving heart for God and for people that made her a loving person and a great encourager. No matter how rough my day was when we spoke she would always manage to see a bright side. I learned through her who I was as a child of God. We had many a Bible study time on the phone. She used to call them our 'evening sacrifice'. Every matter became a matter for prayer, and she prayed without ceasing. I never heard her say, "I am going to pray for you," but always, "Let's pray about this now." I learned from her to seize the moment and to look beyond my own under-standing to get God's perspective on any situation. Dawn helped me to learn the truth that Jesus was concerned with everything about me whether I was caring for Nathan – playing with him or giving him a bath – cooking a meal or taking care of my family. Everything that I was doing in carrying out my responsibilities as a mom, were acts of worship.

Raising Nathan

This helped me in making peace with where I was and impacted my understanding of the responsibility that I carried, not just as a mother and a wife but also as a child of God.

Once when I had fallen into a frenzy, feeling inadequate in my walk as a budding Christian and that I was not doing enough for God because of the load of my familial responsibilities, Dawn listened to my tirade for a while. When I grew silent, in a matter-of-fact conversational tone she said, "Tell me something Chrissy, when you are thirsty can Nathan get you a drink of water?" I thought, why is she asking me a question for which she already knows the answer and why is she asking me such a foolish question, what does it have to do with what I just shared with her? "No," I answered. She continued, "Can Nathan rub your tired feet after you have been running around all day taking care of your family?" Again I answered, "No." "Can he call Mr Ebanks (which is how she always referred to Robert) for you?" "No," I responded. "So," she continued, "If Nathan cannot do anything for you, why do you love him?" "I love him because he is my baby – I love him not for what he can do for me but because I am his mom." I could hear her smiling over the phone as she said, "That is exactly it. The same way you love Nathan not because of anything that he can do for you or give you that is how God loves you. You don't have to do a thing to earn His love. Him jus' love you." That got me thinking. Then just like that she switched from her 'teacher hat' to her 'friend hat' and lightened the mood with a joke. We spoke some more after that and by the time she hung up my anxiety had abated.

Those hours spent talking with Dawn helped me to begin the slow climb back up from the deep pit of despair I had settled into. I was so caught up in my own situation that I never once thought about what she must have had to give up, in order to become the physical manifestation of the grace of God to me. Like clockwork her call came in at 6pm Monday to Sunday. She said that she didn't want to cut in on Mr Ebank's family time so she called well before she knew he would be home from work. Always she would start off our conversations with, "Where is Mr Ebanks?" On the occasions when Robert came home while I was on the phone once she heard his voice, and it didn't matter what we were discussing, her response would be, "Is that Mr Ebanks? Tell him good night for me. Talk to you later Chrissy, I don't want to impose on Mr Ebanks' time." And just like that she was gone. Dawn never got the opportunity to marry but she taught me to not take my husband for granted and to honour him with my attention. I now believe that this teaching from her helped to hold my marriage together during this very difficult and dark period of our lives.

Little by little I began to pull myself together. I could still not see the way forward but I was not prepared to sit where I was anymore. I was tired of being sad, tired of feeling useless and helpless and worthless, and tired of feeling like a hand out. I wanted my independence back.

Nathan was now almost three years old and the impact of his disability had grown more pronounced. I had to do something. And so I organized an event management workshop called, 'The A to Z of Event Management' – Dawn was my biggest cheerleader. I held the workshop in February of 2007. It was moderately successful and I made new contacts that would serve me well in the future. It also provided me with enough funds to purchase a laptop – my first post-diagnosis investment in a new life.

Chapter 28
A Ray of Hope

A few weeks before Nathan's third birthday, I reached another defining moment. The work that I was doing with him had hit another plateau. He had outgrown everything that I had learned to do and I could see that he wanted to do more, but I was at a loss and didn't know where to turn. I resorted to driving around Kingston and St Andrew knocking on every door that I saw with a disability sign but no one could help us. My frustration was high – I had left my job to work with Nathan and I could not help him. In desperation I turned to the Internet and before long I found some great information on cerebral palsy and its management. I realized that if I was to help my son then I needed to take him somewhere where there were many children like him, to a facility that had a success rate of working with such children. I read that Nathan needed a comprehensive assessment with an interdisciplinary team of specialists. I needed to take him overseas to the United States.

Raising Nathan

I phoned my mom in Miami and Olive, another of my
sisters, and together their help enabled me to locate a
developmental paediatrician in Sunrise, Florida. I
called the doctor's office and her secretary said that
they had a waiting list for appointments of a year. I
told her I didn't have a year for my son and something
happened because she asked me to stay on hold and
came back to ask if we could get there by the middle
of March, less than a week away. I made the appointment, got off the phone and prayed.

I called an emergency meeting with Robert and he
took the rest of the day off so that we could go to Hope
Gardens in St. Andrew to talk. I told him all that I had
learned and what I wanted to do and we agreed to
approach his parents for help. I was very nervous
because what we needed was quite a large sum of
money. Furthermore from what I had read Nathan
needed to see at least seven specialists but I only had
one appointment. Robert's parents agreed to meet
with us and I laid out my plans and how much it would
cost. Having not grown up with a father in my life I
got my first glimpse of the true image of a father with
Robert's Dad's next response. When I had finished
speaking he said, "When do you want to leave?"

It was Saturday and I said by Wednesday. He then said, "Since you need the funds in US dollars, I will give it to you by Monday evening. Go ahead and book your tickets." I exhaled. My heart was overwhelmed with gratitude. I was able to understand a father's love for his son and grandson. I also understood then that Nathan's paternal grandparents were as vested in Nathan's wellbeing as we were, and as my mom and sister Jennifer were. I was not as alone as I had thought.

The arrangements to leave went smoothly. The plan was for us to stay with my mom and Olive. The paediatrician's office in Sunrise was almost three hours from where my sister lived. However, my mom and I mapped it out and she made the journey by bus before I arrived so we would know exactly where we needed to go.

I took a leap of faith and left on the Wednesday with Nathan and Adrianne in tow. I was taking Adrianne with me to help with Nathan, plus she was 11 years old going on 40 and she seemed to be having a difficult time with the onset of puberty coupled with all the changes that were happening in our family. We found that she didn't seem to separate well from me for any length of time, so I brought her along because I realized that she needed her mom. We were lucky as just as I was about to enter the customs line at Miami International an elderly customs officer approached and took us to the special assistance line because I was traveling with two children including a toddler in a wheelchair. Olive had come to meet us and I followed her home in a rental car – it was a harrowing experience as it was my first time behind the wheel in a foreign country! But we arrived at her house safely where I prepared for our appointment the very next day.

We were scheduled to see Dr Lucy Cohen, a Developmental Pediatrician and Psychiatrist at her office in Healthsouth Rehabilitation Centre, Cutler Bay. We set out at 5:00am and arrived at the facility at about 8:45am, and freshened up in the car before heading in to register Nathan. I didn't know what I was expecting to see but I was pleasantly surprised. The hospital was large, brightly lit and spacious. Everything was so clean and cheerful, it made me feel good to be there. There were about half a dozen children with their parents in the waiting room – all of the children were in wheelchairs. What particularly appealed to me was that they all looked healthy and happy, bright-eyed and 'bushy-tailed'! Each of their chairs were state of the art wheelchairs, fully loaded with trays and gadgets hanging off them. As we waited they took sips of water or juice from beautiful child-friendly, spill-proof cups with built in straws. Each child was wearing ankle foot orthotics (AFOS) which were almost knee high with characters on them such as Sponge Bob, Sesame Street and Dora the Explorer. They made disability look cool! Being in their company, however, made me incredibly sad for Nathan who was sitting in a baby stroller that he had long outgrown and was clearly not comfortable in. We were using a kiddie's cup to pour juice and water down his throat because he could not suck through a straw. And his clothes were all in dark colours because I had not paid much thought to putting bright colours in his wardrobe. I felt like a failure. I also felt sorry for every child with a disability in Jamaica. I asked myself, "What makes our children any less deserving that these children?" "Why don't the children back home have anything like this?"

I had become used to sterile and unfriendly office spaces for children with disabilities so I was wonderfully surprised when we entered Dr Cohen's office – it was like a kids' wonderland! I was also impressed with her bedside manner. She greeted me but her eyes were fixed on Nathan and she wore a big smile as if he was her best friend in the whole world and she was very happy to see him. Nathan responded and smiled back at her, babbling happily. She set him in a corner of the room to play on a mat with his sister and then proceeded to extract his full history from me. I had become adept at anticipating these questions and I had taken copies with me of all of his reports and X-rays.

When Dr Cohen had finished the interview she carried out a detailed physical examination of Nathan explaining to me every step of the way what she was doing and why. When the assessment was over she set Nathan back to play with his sister, a task with which he happily complied. Because of our tight timeline Dr Cohen prepared her report within three days following our consultation – we collected it later that week.

Patient Name: *Nathan Ebanks*

DOB: *05/04/04*

Informant: *Patient's mother*

Referring Physician: *Dr Melbourne Chambers, Jamaica*

Records Reviewed: *Some notes from Jamaica*

History:

By report, he is in a special school.

Has been diagnosed with dyskenetic CP and failure to thrive.

MRI was done which reports a normal study.

CAT scan done as a baby showed mild generalized cerebral atrophy.

By report, has some equipment at home and mother is looking for equipment.

He will roll around on his belly and reports to hit his head.

Past Medical Report:

A 36-week gestation. Mother was 39, vaginal delivery, G4, P4-0-0-4, was noted with the congenital diaphragmatic hernia. Day #3 he had repair of the hernia, Day #10 he was jaundiced and hyponatremic, treated.

Birth weight was 5 pounds 8 ounces. Apgar scores were 4/8. No seizures.

Past Surgical History: *Hernia repair.*

Medications: *None.*

Development History: *Rolled over, is unable to sit or walk.*

Activities Of Daily Living:
By report, will finger feed and drinks from a bottle. Eats regular foods and regular liquids. Has home-made stander and gait trainer, goes to STEP Centre for children with multiple disabilities.

Family History:
There are three siblings. There is a cousin who has autism. Mother works as a marketing specialist. Father works as a financial controller.

The report went on to note in detail the tests which were carried out with the following diagnosis:

Tone is diminished.
He is able to reach randomly for an object, tends to use right greater than left and reaches better with

right than left.
Sitting balance is poor.
Standing balance is poor.

Impression:

1. *Hypotonic CP.* [Hypotonia is diminished muscle tone. An infant or child with hypotonic cerebral palsy appears floppy, like a rag doll. In early infancy, hypotonia can be easily spotted by the inability of the child to gain any head control when pulled by the arms to a sitting position – this symptom is often referred to as head lag. Children with severe hypotonia may have the most difficulty of all children with cerebral palsy in attaining motor skill milestones and normal cognitive development.][1]

2. *Failure to thrive.* [Failure to thrive refers to children whose current weight or rate of weight gain is much lower than that of other children of similar age and gender. Failure to thrive may be caused by medical problems or factors in the child's environment, such as abuse or neglect.][2]

Recommendations:

1. *Spent a long time with mother discussing options for equipment. I would recommend the Tomatoe Feeding System, this can be used as a seat, can be also put on the stroller base and a car seat.*

2. *A prone stander.* [A prone stander is used by children able to maintain head control with their anterior trunk supported and their arms placed forward on the tray. The prone stander supports the child from the front of the body; the user is in a forward leaning position and can easily view their activity and surroundings, thus further developing their neck and upper trunk extensor muscles for postural control.]

3. *Benik Vest.* [Benik vests are thick vests usually made of material like neoprene with weights that can be attached at various points to help with posture, balance and core strengthening. They are used to help children develop muscle tone.]

4. *SMOs.* [Sports Medicine Orthopaedics. In Nathan's case – foot braces (ankle feet

orthotics) and arm braces to support him during his standing, walking and arm propping exercises.]

5. *Danmar soft shell helmet.* [Because Nathan had poor head control, he banged his head a lot when he was on the floor or doing any movement. The helmet is like a bicycle helmet intended to protect the head. Nathan never liked anything on his head and so he never consented to wearing the helmet.]

6. *Do not feel that he is a candidate for a walker as yet at this point in time.*

7. *PT, OT, ST evaluation and home exercise programme to be followed back in Jamaica.* [Physical Therapy (PT), Occupational Therapy (OT), Speech Therapy (ST). This was our first ever home management and exercise programme – I felt hopeful for the first time.]

8. *Follow up in six weeks with bracing.*

Signed, Lucy S. Cohen, M.D. LSC: POL-030707-7252457

I left Dr Cohen's office that morning with a shopping list for equipment and referrals to see an Occupational Therapist, Physical Therapist, Orthotist, Nutritionist, Audiologist and an Optometrist. I had information and hope. I felt empowered and for the first time felt that things were going to be alright. It did not enter my mind how we would fit in all these appointments in the two and a half weeks that remained of our visit. But where there is a will there is always a way.

Chapter 29

Where There is a Will,
There is Always a Way

My mom had stayed in the car with Nathan and Adrianne while I went to collect the report from Dr Cohen. I was so glad that she was there to support us. It helped enormously to have someone to talk to about it. I told her that Dr Cohen had said it would take months to set up all the recommended therapies. "But we don't have months," my mom responded. "Let us go to the therapy centre right now and see if the Lord will favour us." So we headed to the Rehabilitation Centre which was just around the corner from Dr Cohen's office.

We walked into a very large, bright and spacious kiddie's gym. I stood still for a moment to drink in the facility. What a pleasant and child-inviting space I thought, and it certainly doesn't look like anything I have seen back home. In that moment I desperately wanted Nathan to be treated by this centre. I was directed to the consultation room and was lucky enough to find the physical therapist, Mary Hamilton, there –

Raising Nathan

I liked her right away. She was pleasant, helpful and most importantly she spoke to Nathan and included him in her conversation with us. Whatever I told her she would turn to him and say, "Nathan, your mommy just told me so and so," or as she suggested what the plan would look like for him, she would turn to him and say, "Nathan, as you just heard, I was sharing with mommy, grandma and your sister that we will need to do so and so..." Mary's attitude particularly impressed me as in all of my experiences back home Nathan had been invisible to most of the specialists who were treating him – I always felt that they lost sight of the fact that they were talking about a young child.

Mary introduced us to Marcia, the occupational therapist. There was a large appointments board behind them and I could see that their schedules were tight. Nonetheless I asked when the first opening was. Mary glanced at the board and said August (which was four and a half months away). I told her that we only had two and a half weeks as we had to return home. Before she could respond a telephone call came in and she excused herself to answer it – a few moments later she returned with a big smile. "Guess what?" she asked, "If you are free right now I can take Nathan. The

call I just got was from my 11:30am client and they
cancelled. Marcia had the same client scheduled for
2pm. I could not believe my ears – we were going to
get the first two therapies that same day!

Mary and Nathan hit it off right away. Later I learned
why. Mary and her husband, who were both strawberry
blond, had adopted a black baby boy who had cerebral
palsy – the child's mother was in prison for drugs
offences. The baby was born prematurely with challenges
and was placed in an early stimulation programme
under state care once he was stabilized enough to be
released from hospital after birth. Mary was assigned
as his therapist. As she told it, she fell in love with him,
and she and her husband adopted him when he was
nine months old. She worked with him day and night
mixing sports medicine with traditional therapy and
pretty much just throwing everything she could at him.
She told me that one day when he had just turned
three she was at home and her mother had phoned.
She jokingly told her son to come to the phone to talk
to nana and was shocked when he got up and walked
slowly but purposefully to take the phone from her
hand. She said she just started screaming, laughing,
crying, hugging and kissing him. I was inspired.

Raising Nathan

Mary completed Nathan's assessment and then rearranged her schedule to make as many appointments as she could to see him over the next two weeks – most of the appointments were during her lunch times. She also informed me that since I had no insurance the hospital had an 'out of pocket' discount. The full cost of each session was United States $588. The out of pocket discount was 50 percent. I was very grateful and delighted for the tip. 'Out of pocket' became my precursor to every conversation from then onwards! Although it does not make a difference in Jamaica it has worked in most places in the United States. The discount meant we could organize twice the number of services for Nathan.

Though Nathan obviously grew to adore Mary very quickly he still screamed and had tantrums throughout the physical therapy assessment and the subsequent exercise programmes. And the occupational therapy sessions were no different. I was not perturbed because I knew that this was good for him. I was also amazed at how developed his lungs had become!

When we were finished on the first day, Mary got on the phone and called each of the other services that we were hoping to see. I sat and listened to her cajoling appointments for us with every one. The orthotist was about to go on vacation and she talked him into meeting us at a colleagues facility the following evening before leaving for his flight. We left the Rehabilitation Centre that evening with appointments for every service on Dr Cohen's list. That was indeed a divine intervention!

For the next two weeks we were on the road from 5am every morning to 11pm at night from Monday straight through to Friday, as we crammed in every scheduled appointment and some new appointments which came up along the way.

Nathan's hearing assessment was confirmed with Audiology Associates of South Florida – a 30 minute drive from Dr Cohen's office and a three and a half hour drive from my sister's home. My mother had already left for Canada to visit Vivienne, another of my sisters, so it was now just Nathan, Adrianne and I. Adrianne was a really good travel companion and a great sister. Having her there helped a lot as I became bone tired from all the driving. We often got lost but always managed to find our way in the end.

We received the audiology report on March 13th. The report stated:

> *Auditory brainstem response testing could only be completed for the right ear as he (Nathan) woke up during the testing for the left ear. There was no wave V response at the maximum level (90dBHL) in the right ear confirming the presence of a severe to profound hearing loss.*

> **Impression**: *Responses obtained demonstrate a bilateral, severe to profound sensorineural, hearing loss.*

A hearing aid evaluation for binaural amplification was recommended for as soon as possible but there was no time for any further testing because of our limited schedule and so earmolds were made in order to fit Nathan with hearing aids. The prescription was put on rush and we were able to have them fitted the day before our departure.

Something about the hearing assessment did not sit well with me. While it was true that Nathan did not appear to respond to noise, and I sat through the full hearing tests and saw his lack of responses, I had a feeling deep down that his hearing was intact. I was too shy to share this with the doctor and so went along with the recommended action.

Nathan knew there was nothing wrong with his hearing and from day one he refused to keep the hearing aids in. It became a wearying dance putting an aid in one ear only to have him grab it out and throw it to the floor by the time I got the other ear fitted! We battled for the rest of the trip and for another two weeks at home. Then, on a very rare occasion, I got him to keep them in his ears one Saturday morning. I had just stepped away when a loud explosion rang out – the electrical transformer at the end of our street had blown out. The hearing aids must have amplified the sound because Nathan was startled and almost jumped clear out of his chair! He grabbed both aids (the first time he'd used his hands simultaneously), ripped them from his ears and threw them to the ground. He never allowed us to put them in again from that day on... because he has never needed them!

I noticed a change in Nathan's hearing right away. A few hours after the noise incident, our dog, Lion, made a sudden sharp bark outside under the window where Nathan was sitting. Nathan jumped for the second time to a noise... I could see in his eyes that he was startled and excited. He was recognizing a strange sound for the first time. So I quickly told him, "That was our dog, Lion, he was barking." Nathan smiled as if he understood. After that I made it a daily point of duty to talk to him and make different sounds from different directions around him. From a, "Psst," to a whisper, to calling his name, to shouting, clapping, stomping, banging forks together and so on. At first he would look in the direction of the sound but after a while he realized that it was not a big deal so he stopped looking. However I could still see the slight turn of his head in the direction of the noise, or the sudden blink of his eyes in response to the sound. There was no doubt that he was hearing and hearing well. Today when a noise is too loud like people's chatter, a honking horn or a barking dog, he covers both of his ears with his hands and with his special 'babble-talk', he tells the noise to shut up!

What this whole experience taught me was that while there is a place for expert assessments and opinions, parents and families play just as important a role in observing behaviour. Particularly where speech is absent in the child, parents observations help to qualify what is going on to make a more accurate picture. In Nathan's case a local audiologist in Kingston pointed out that it seemed that there was not anything wrong structurally with Nathan's hearing but rather that the brain stem that controls his hearing was not developed. We can't be sure what exactly contributed to the eventual development but if I had not observed the change the hearing aids may have created 'noise-induced deafness'. Today Nathan's 'superman' hearing is one of his biggest strengths. I kept the hearing aids as a souvenir, a United States $2,050 souvenir, before finally donating them to the Jamaica Association for the Deaf in about 2012.

A Speech and Language Pathology (SLP) assessment was next. This was held back at the Healthsouth Rehabilitation Centre with a therapist called Stacy. The Preschool Language Scale: 4th Edition was used to assess Nathan's total language abilities. It has an average score of 100 with a standard deviation of +/- 15. Nathan obtained the following scores:

Subtest	Standard Score (SS)	Percentile Rank	Age Equivalent
Auditory Comprehension	53	1	1 year 1 month
Expressive Communication	52	1	11 months
Total Language	50	1	11 months

He was almost three years old when the assessment was done. The bad news was that Nathan was diagnosed with a severe to profound speech and language disorder marked by total language ability which fell three standard deviations below the norm, and he had an inability to produce a variety of age appropriate phonemes, syllables and words.

The good news was that the report went on to say that his potential for improvement was good based on family participation and early intervention – we were provided with a gruelling schedule of language

stimulation routines to carry out on a daily basis.
Continued treatment via skilled speech pathology
services was recommended as necessary to assist in
the remediation and deficits. This last statement
deflated my hope – where would I find a speech
therapist back home?

Upon my return home I discovered to my disappointment that there were very few speech and language
pathologists on the island and the few who were here
were overworked and overbooked. Regrettably in all
the years – and Nathan is almost 11 now – we have
never been able to carry out this recommendation
in Jamaica.

We had a follow up appointment with Dr Cohen and
Nathan also had his eye assessment. He was seen by
Dr Mary Bartuccio, the Assistant Professor at Nova
Southeastern University's College of Optometry on
May 5th, the day following his birthday. The assessment
report stated that Nathan had 'optic nerve pallor'
[severe visual impairment] in both eyes, and recom-
mended that he be evaluated by a paediatric ophthalmol-
ogist so that his visual prognosis could be determined.
The doctor also recommended stimulation activities to

further enhance Nathan's visual system. The doctor suggested that Nathan be encouraged to play games on the floor like rolling or crawling activities (he never did learn how to crawl), as well as picking up small food objects such as Cheerios, cereal, or sweet treats – and so started my first training in carrying out visual stimulation activities. The aim of the exercise was to encourage Nathan to look at the target before grabbing it. Because Nathan had a preference for using his right side the doctor recommended that we place food in his left field of view to encourage the awareness of his visual field on that side. We were given a six month appointment to return to monitor his progress, vision and his eye skills. But we never returned, we were unable to raise the funds to do so.

Nathan's development exploded that year. He now had the recommended equipment and he had a wide range of colourful sensory and tactile toys. My knowledge and skills grew exponentially as did my confidence in working with him. On the recommendation of the physical therapist, Mary, we withdrew Nathan from his current school to enrol him in a mainstream school. Mary had told me that she felt that this was the best option for Nathan as she believed that he had above average intelligence. While she was working with him she carried out some cognitive assessments and had seen that Nathan demonstrated age appropriate skills cognitively. His deficit was not with his receptive language and comprehension skills but rather with his weak functional and expressive language skills. I will never forget it when she said that, **"We should place Nathan where his mind was and not where his skill was."** This was the second piece of advice that was a catalyst in changing my view of disability and the expectations that I had for my son.

Between then and 2011 I took Nathan to the United States four times for short bouts of speech and language interventions. But it was not enough to produce the development of which I knew Nathan was capable. It broke my heart to know that after all he had been through and all the effort and money we poured into his development he did not have a fair chance to pursue his potential because he had been born and was living in a developing nation where these services are not readily available.

Within three weeks of our return home Nathan had achieved all of his short, mid and long term goals.

Raising Nathan

My knowledge had again plateaued and I realized that we needed another trip. His grandfather kindly funded it again and in May we made a second visit to the United States. This time my sister Jennifer came with me and we stayed at a hotel next door to the Healthsouth Centre – mom came up to visit us for a day. All the specialists were amazed with Nathan's achievements. He was given his second set of long term goals. He achieved all at an exponential rate, however, we were not able to take him back for a third visit. The gap planted the seed of starting an organization to facilitate this type of support, as we recognized then that we needed to help bridge the gap for this kind of support.

Chapter 30
Bridging the Gap

Nowhere was the impact of Nathan's disabilities and his accompanying special needs more evident than in school. In the earlier years when he was enrolled at the school for special needs children, I was as enthusiastic about him going to school as I was with his siblings. In my mind he was a child and children should be in school. Nathan attending school also gave me a sense that Nathan was fitting in, in spite of his condition. Most of the people I had spoken to, including his neurologist, did not feel that school was necessary for him. One professional even advised me, "You should not be concerned with using your money to send him to school because he will never learn." Closing my mind to all that negativity was the only way that I could cope with the situation and we enrolled him into the special needs school to bring some normality into his life and ours.

I returned to Jamaica after that second visit determined to follow through with Dr Mary's recommendation, but I was not sure where to begin the process. I knew what I needed to do and that I needed to move quickly to get Nathan in a regular education programme. I just did not know where to start. I became consumed with the idea of Nathan attending a regular school but while the thought excited me it also scared me. Was that the right decision for my child? Would I find a school that would take him? What if we gave up his space and then couldn't find another school for him? Would the other children accept him or tease him? What if he wasn't smart enough to manage? While I had many questions I knew that I had to initiate the process as there was a notice period that I had to give to his current school. So at the end of that school term we took another leap of faith, we gave notice to take Nathan out of his current school.

The week before the start of the new school term we had still not found a school for Nathan – it was also time for his siblings to return to regular schooling. I got into the car and started driving from my neighbourhood in Stony Hill down into Constant Spring Square. As I got to the traffic lights at the intersection of Constant Spring Road and Olivier Road I turned left onto Oliver Road though I still did not know where I was heading. I drove for a short distance more and as I approached the former private school of my other children I felt an urgency to turn in through the gates and so I did. I drove into the car park turned off the engine and sat for a moment. I looked around and asked myself, "What are you doing here? Have you not heard that the school is full and there is no space?" Despite this internal dialog, I got out of the car and started heading towards the administrative office. As I got halfway up the steps I saw the school's principal. She greeted me with some warmth and asked if I was back in Jamaica. When we had withdrawn our three eldest children the September before, it was with the intention of migrating to Canada. I explained that those plans had not worked out and that we had been in Jamaica all along and the children were being home schooled by a friend. I told her that I wanted them to return to regular schooling and she asked if I was sending them back to her school. When I told her that I had heard that the school was full she replied, "Mrs Ebanks, I am sure we can find space for your children." I was delighted but still apprehensive because I did not see how we could afford the school fees with me no longer being employed, in addition we would need school uniforms for all three children and books in time for the summer term just one week away.

I shared these concerns with her and she said, "Don't worry about it, we can work something out." I then said to her, "Great, now all I have to do is to find a school for Nathan." She asked me what I meant and I explained that the physical therapist we had seen in Florida recommended that we get him into a regular school. She thought about it for about a second and then made me an offer that sent my heart jumping for joy, she said, "We are not equipped to cater to Nathan's needs, but if you are willing to try and can find a 'shadow' to send to school with him, I would be willing to take him in." Never in a thousand years would I have even considered that possibility and nor would I have asked. I saw the whole experience as the providential hand of God and so I gladly and quickly took up the offer.

I drove home that afternoon to share the good news with Nathan and the rest of my family. In my head I made a tick on the checklist by the 'find Nathan a school' entry. My mind now moved on to the second hurdle – to find Nathan a compatible nanny to accompany him to school. This was a tall order in my mind because up to that point my experience of people looking after Nathan had not been good.

I did not know where to start with the recruitment process. I profiled the person I needed for him – a female between 20 and 30 years old. I reasoned that although I was in my early 40s and filled with energy, Nathan still wore me down. So it was important that the person was young so that she could keep up with him; was strong enough to do the lifting required; and adaptable enough to be a quick learner.

I immediately started the search by calling people I knew and trusted to ask if they knew anyone. Next I called two of the leading programmes which trained practical nurses but had no success with them. A recruitment agency was recommended and I telephoned and spoke with the manager. After explaining in depth exactly what kind of person we were looking for, the manager said she had three people who would be ideal and so I scheduled for them to come to my home at different times the following day for an interview. Someone I knew heard that I was in the market for a nanny for Nathan and recommended a former school mate of theirs to me. Within twenty-four hours I had four candidates lined up for interviews.

The first person scheduled did not show up. That was fine with me – it was better she didn't show up now than for her not to be present when she needed to be at school. The second person arrived about 20 minutes late. I was standing on my veranda looking out for her when I saw this middle-aged woman puffing her way up the street. I did not pay much attention as I had been very specific about the age range I was looking for. When the woman stopped at my gate I realized that she was my 11am interviewee. I opened the gate for her and watched with some bemusement as she struggled up the gently sloped driveway. She appeared to be in her late fifties or early sixties and weighed about 250lbs. Sweat was pouring from her body. She paused to rest at the bottom of the steps leading up to the veranda before she began the slow and painful climb, wincing as she made each step. I knew she would not be suitable but thought the decent thing to do would be to conduct the interview since she had made the effort to come.

She finally made it to the top of the brief flight of stairs and hung on to the grill, out of breath and panting for a few seconds, before saying her hello! I offered her a seat and a glass of water before commencing. At no point did she apologize for her lateness, I don't think she even realized that she was late – another reason she was not suitable. We had barely gotten started with the interview when her mobile phone rang. Without even as much as an excuse she answered, "'ello!" She listened to the person on the other end and then responded, "Wha? But me nevva say dat! A lie she a tell pan me!" I was flabbergasted. She continued with her phone call, oblivious that I was sitting there conducting an interview with her. She chatted for two to three minutes and then told the person, "Me wi call yuh lata." That was my cue. Getting up from my seat I said, "Thank you Miss 'N', that will be all." She struggled out of the chair and turned to me and asked, "Then meh get the jab?" I said to her, "Well it is still early days I have other people to interview so I will notify your agency when I've made my decision." She left and as I watched her hobble away I struck her name from my list.

Raising Nathan

The next candidate was a big improvement over the one who didn't show and Miss N! She was a very pleasant young lady, 25 years old, who seemed eager to get the job. I reviewed her references and as I conducted the interview my three older children kept peeking around the door onto the veranda. Satisfied with the answers I received she was in a running position for the job. I gave her the final test. I went inside the house got Nathan and brought him back to the veranda. I introduced him to her and then asked her to hold him for a minute to see what Nathan's sixth sense made of her. I made the request casually but I was very alert and watchful of the interaction. Miss 'W' took Nathan and immediately began to talk to him. Nathan sat looking into her face for a few minutes before slowly settling. He did not seem convinced one way or another but I felt she had passed the test. I put a tick beside her name and informed her that a decision would be made by the end of the day and if she was shortlisted she would be called in to meet with my husband before a final decision would be made.

I was down to the final interview and Tasinena arrived on time – she was softly spoken and appeared to be very shy. From the moment I saw her there was a connection. The older children seemed to take to her as well – I later learned that it was hard for Tasinena to hold a straight face as they came darting past the doorway behind my back, clowning around for her amusement.

Satisfied with the formal part of the interview it was now time for the Nathan test. I got Nathan from inside and before I could hand him to her he reached for her, looked into her face, flashed her his million dollar smile, wrapped his arms around her neck and lay his head on her shoulder. It was as if he had known her all of his life. By the end of that week she was hired and her orientation began the week after. By the time the new term began, Nathan went to his new school with his new nanny.

Then I moved on to the next big question, how were we going to afford all of this – Nathan's school fees, books and his nanny's salary?

Raising Nathan

Chapter 31

A New Beginning

Nathan started school in April 2007 in the Kindergarten 2 classroom – there was one other child in the class with mild disabilities. His teacher, Mrs 'D', loved him right from the start. She told me she had a niece to whom she said she was very close who had autism. She felt that having Nathan in her classroom was God's way of showing her that she had a special mission for children with special needs.

Nathan's integration into the new school environment went much better than we expected. He spent his first days just sitting and watching his classmates and teachers. His classmates didn't seem to notice that he was different from them – they were excited about pushing his chair around and were overly helpful when he needed to be moved. They flocked to him, showing him toys and explaining things when he didn't seem to know. Mrs D was wonderful. Each day she would great me with the words, "I am still waiting to see his special needs. Today he did everything that two and a half year olds do. Sorry Mrs Ebanks, but there was nothing special about his needs today." She would say it with a smile. This was a wonderful booster for me and Nathan settled into his new environment very quickly.

Tasinena was very good with Nathan. She was a very resourceful and highly creative young woman. Long before we began exposing her to special education practices and tools she would spend time throughout the day reviewing tasks that Nathan had difficulty completing trying to work out how they could be modified to give Nathan increased access. For the next five years she became my strong right hand person and one of Nathan's biggest cheerleaders. Tasinena was Nathan's caregiver at home, his companion on long trips, his playmate, teaching assistant and friend. He loved her fiercely and she him. He brought out the best in her and helped her to discover latent talents. So it was not unexpected that within a few weeks Nathan began to thrive and show significant development.

One of the activities that Nathan's class did each morning was to allow children who arrived early to play with toys – many of them gravitated to the building blocks and Lego. When the bell rang for the school day to begin the children also began a 'clean up activity'. To our wonder and joy, within a short time frame Nathan also began to participate. Tasinena would put a basket in front of him and he would put the toys he was playing with in the basket. He actually looked forward to this activity and we were overjoyed as we witnessed explosive growth and development in his packing and stacking skills, because this was an activity that he fought having to do in therapy. He also began to absorb age-typical behaviours as he modelled his peers. What we did not account for, however, was that he would also model 'naughty' behaviour such as spitting, begging and my least favourite, hitting and pinching. We struggled with applauding him and reprimanding him and unfortunately for his siblings these conflicting messages fuelled bad behaviour for quite some time.

Nathan completed the term in Kindergarten 2 and was promoted to Kindergarten 3 at which point his experience of school took a bad turn. His teacher Mrs 'G' was a nice lady but Nathan did not have the requisite skills needed to function in the new environment and the teacher did not have the necessary skills to help him or to modify and adapt teaching practices or materials. In fairness to the teacher she was interested but was out of her depth. This triggered an all too familiar feeling, it was time for me to intervene once again. I had come to learn over the years that the only way Nathan would get even a smidgen of what he needed would be if I sourced it, provided or created it for him. As the school term progressed I watched as the light from his eyes slowly died. He no longer liked school but he did not want to stay at home either.

Nathan's teacher later confessed that she was scared to have him in her class initially because she did not know what to do with him. She said that when she spoke to him he did not respond, not even so much of a blink to acknowledge that he heard her. She was convinced that it was either that he could not hear well or he did not understand. I was convinced other-wise and saw that this was Nathan's way of protesting at the changes in his schedule and class. K2 was the fun class and K3 was the 'big kid's' class where he was expected to sit still and do his work. Nathan was not ready for that – not because he could not do the work but because he was a kid. Having survived all that he had gone through in his young life it was no wonder

that at three years old, he was not ready to take life
so seriously.

So much to the discomfort of his poor teacher, Nathan
would strive to do the opposite of everything she told
him to do. At the beginning of this behaviour I too
questioned his cognitive ability. I felt guilty that I was
trying to push him along an academic path. There
were many days when other teachers would gather
just outside the classroom (while Tasinena was inside
struggling to help Nathan complete a task) and ask
Nathan's teacher why she was pushing him to do what
he obviously couldn't do. Nathan would hear them
and a sadness would come into his eyes. Sometimes
he was trying his best to do the activity but his motor
limitations got in the way and when the teachers were
discouraging, he would just give up on the activity. My
heart broke daily for my child but I took him to school
with an outward expression of joyfulness every day.

Over the duration of the time that Nathan was at the
school he developed a number of friendships with
students across all grade levels, parents and the canteen
administrator. In the morning as either Robert or
I wheeled him into school I could see other parents

watching silently. Some smiled warmly, others gave us a look of sympathy, and there were those whose eyes spoke volumes and screamed at us, "Why do you insist on bringing him here, don't you see he shouldn't be here!" I would paint a smile on my face and strut like I was the 'Queen of Sheba' and my son the 'Crown Prince'. I often left school and went home to cry but I was determined to be strong for my child. Over time just by being present and participating in school life, Nathan became a fixture and slowly without ever speaking a word, won over the hearts of many parents, teachers and children.

Chapter 32

Reflection: If I Knew Then What I Know Now

As a parent of a child with disabilities knowledge is empowerment. It is important for us to understand the rights of our child and the laws related to these rights. Like I did, very often we yield all of our rights to the professionals who provide the various services such as in this case, a paediatrician, neurologist or therapist. One of the early lessons I learned concerning this is that as the parent I am with my child 24/7. I know my child and while I may not understand the medical implications of his condition, I am an essential part of his team. Over the course of my child's life he will come in contact with scores of specialists, and when he gets into school age, the professional team will expand to include special education teacher, his classroom teacher (if he is in mainstream schooling) and so on. All of these individuals are transient – they will come and go, but my husband and I, his parents and siblings are the only ones who will be in his life permanently. We hold the key to his support and care, but in order for us to do so, we must become informed, educated and skilled in carrying out the programmes that are set.

In Jamaica there are laws that guarantee the protection, care for the rights of all children, including each child's right to appropriate and equitable education. These include the National Policy for Persons with Disabilities which was tabled in Jamaica Parliament on September 26th 2000. The policy was one of the first consultative documents with the objective of enlightening Jamaicans about disability issues. It provided the first formal blueprint to the country to make further gains towards the inclusion of persons with disabilities in every sphere of Jamaican life. Specifically, the National Policy for Persons with Disabilities:

1. Established guidelines and directions for the government, for the equalization of opportunities for people with disabilities.

2. Provided the first local framework for agencies of government to cooperate in developing and implementing policies designed to provide equal opportunities for people with disabilities in all aspects of life.

3. Assisted government in implementing the United Nations Standard Rules on the equalization of opportunities for persons with disabilities.

4. Served as a precedent to the Disability Act.

Seven years later, in 2007, Jamaica signed and ratified the UN Convention of the Rights of Persons with Disabilities. Thus began the long uphill trek from exclusion to inclusion for persons with disabilities, which would see the passing of the [Jamaica] Disability Act in October 2014, more than 14 years later.

The Disability Act is a civil rights legislation that prohibits discrimination against individuals with disabilities in all areas of public life including jobs, schools, transportation and all public and private places that are open to the general public. The purpose of the legislation is to make sure that people with disabilities have the same rights and opportunities as everyone else in society, among other things. This is a significant piece of landmark legislation for persons with disabilities in Jamaica and signalled a turning point in the nation's knowledge of its responsibility to all its people.

Raising Nathan

For the first time since my son was diagnosed I felt more hopeful for his future. The authorities are now going through public consultation to develop the codes of practice and the regulations that will govern the Act and any day now the minister with responsibility for this portfolio will announce the day this Act will come into law. I can't wait.

Another lesson learned is that when parents know the services to which their child is entitled it helps them to access the services and care that are needed. Such knowledge is vital enough that having it can save, while a lack of such knowledge can result in death.

Raising a child with any disability affects the whole family – the family is the greatest support for the child. On the day we took Nathan home from the hospital the matron who was on duty and who had worked with Nathan gave me some advice. She told me that Nathan would be fragile for a long time to come but that his siblings were the greatest gift we could have given him. She warned that we should not withhold Nathan from them but should teach them from day one how to hold him and help us to take care of him. I followed her advice and later I was very glad that I did.

Reflection: If I Knew Then What I Know Now

One day when Nathan was about six months old I was talking with a neighbour. It was during the summer holidays and the children were all at home. They kept calling out for me and I kept telling them I would be there in a minute. Finally Jordanne ran outside to me and said, "Don't worry mommy, you don't need to come, we did it by ourself." Of course I ran in to find that Nathan had made a bowel movement and the three little kids had worked together to expertly change his diaper (nappy)!

Each of them loves their brother with all of their heart and over the years distinct roles have emerged. Adrianne the eldest who is now 19 years old, carries out much of Nathan's daily caregiving roles – bathing, dressing etc. Watching her with him brings tears to my eyes because of the love and care that she pours on him. Jordanne who is 15 years old, is Nathan's teacher. She does his homework with him and other school related activities. She intuitively adapts his work so that she can capture his input and answer, and she makes working together fun. She stated a few years back that she wants to be a teacher and I think that helping her brother has had something to do with her decision. Ryan who is 17 years old does much of the heavy lifting, carrying Nathan or his wheelchair up and down the stairs, and cleaning his wheelchair. He also does the rough play with Nathan, something Nathan looks forward to as I learned once when I tried to stop them. Over the years our family became organized around Nathan's needs and this has helped to increase his confidence, his security and knowledge that we love and appreciate him very much.

I have learned many lessons about advocacy. As parents we naturally speak for our child. I have always been a hands-on mother who was not afraid to represent my child's voice and interest in any forum. Yet when I received Nathan's diagnosis I lost all confidence in myself. I thought that this was outside of my knowledge and ability and I began to depend solely on the 'experts' – doctors and therapists. I did not dream of making any decisions for him even after I'd seen that my instincts were right. I was so bent on 'fixing' my son that I trusted everyone with a specialist name and every programme I heard about wholeheartedly – and did not question anything. After the first wave of disappointment when things didn't go the way I envisioned I began to see the need to learn. There were also times when I did not follow my mind and things turned out badly.

In my journey to have confidence in myself and my choices I remember that Nathan's paediatrician, Dr Andrea Dewdney, was the first medical professional to give me the opportunity to test drive my instincts. Nathan was ill for a few weeks with a fever and congestion and was not responding to treatment. I sat in Dr Dewdney's office for the umpteenth time. She asked me a simple question, she said, "Mrs Ebanks, normally I would not give a child who is typically developed antibiotics, but with Nathan I don't want to take the chance and not give him something. I don't want a repeat of the pneumonia experience. What do you think?" I was taken aback. None of the doctors and specialists had ever solicited my opinion or input. I told her that I thought she was 'spot on' in needing to give Nathan antibiotics and she then made the decision. We saw the change in him within 24 hours, and in less than a week he was as right as rain. The experience helped me to realize that my opinion mattered.

From then onwards I became fully engaged in my son's life. I became a part of every decision. With every test or assessment done I collected a copy of the report and findings for my file and kept the documents carefully organized. I was no longer afraid to ask questions when I didn't know. I made myself an integral part of his team. There were times when I came across professionals who were threatened and refused to get my opinion. After trying to reason with them, if there was still a barrier, I changed the service.

Through my advocacy work I have learned that children depend on their parents and families to be as informed and empowered as they can be. Families should create a vision and build inclusive lives for their children. No one can tell you what that should mean. The first time a therapist asked me what the goal was that I had for my son, I thought this was the dumbest question ever. "To walk!" was my response. It was later that I learned that wasn't the question she was asking. Her question was, "What hurts your heart and breaks your back?"[1] She wanted to know what were the little things with which I would like help; things such as Nathan being able to push himself out of his wheelchair when I was taking him out so that I didn't have to hurt my back bending picking up his whole weight; or being able to lift up Nathan's bottom from the bed when I was taking off his trousers; or Nathan being able to sit upright, so that I could see to feed him. Those were the goals that she was talking about, but at that time I did not have a vision of the parts which made up the whole. I knew the end product I wanted to see in Nathan's life, but I did not know the steps that were needed to get him there. As a result, my expectation of the therapist's interventions were unrealistic. She did end up setting us some more achievable goals, but I did not then understand their significance and I felt cheated.

So it is important that families create a vision and be the driver in building inclusive lives for their child. What is your vision for your child? Ours for Nathan as with each of his siblings is that Nathan will be self-sufficient, make choices, have meaningful relationships, find and fulfil his God-given purpose and give back to the community. Once the vision is created and agreed the next step is to share the vision with your child's team – the child themself, everyone at home, at school, the paediatrician and therapy team (if your child has one). Your vision must be used to guide daily activities and gear the child towards future goals.

Raising Nathan

Chapter 33

From Emotions to Advocacy

Parents are often the best advocates for their children, especially when the child has a disability or special need. When you speak up for your child you do so as a parent-advocate. True, advocacy is largely a positive process which should build on your child's strengths and achievements. As your child's best advocate you are in a unique position to identify and implement positive changes. To develop and strengthen your advocacy skills you must:

- Get a comprehensive evaluation (disabilities and disorders of any sort are complex and at times confusing). Effective treatment and management depends on a careful and accurate diagnosis – a full assessment often involves several visits.

- Ask lots of questions about any diagnosis or proposed treatment. Remember that no one has all the answers.

- Insist on care that is 'family centered' and builds on your child's strengths. Ask about specific goals and objectives. How will you know if treatment is helping? If your child's problems persist or worsen what options and alternatives are available?

- Get to know the rules. What are the laws, policies and eligibility criteria that drive you? What services does your child need and why?

- Get to know the people who make decisions about your child's development and education. Whether your child attends school or day care, talk with his or her teacher, visit the classroom and observe your child's day from time to time. If possible volunteer in the classroom and volunteer to assist with school functions. I volunteered for every committee I could at my children's schools. I volunteered to be President of the PTA and served ferociously, it helped to keep my mind off of my dilemma.

- Keep records – this is one thing that I learned from my mother. It is important that as parents we maintain organized medical and educational records and assessment information. Make note-taking a part of your routine. Take notes during telephone conversations and face to face meetings. Ask for people's full names and contact information when communicating by telephone or by email. Keep a journal with samples of your child's work and academic progress such as homework, papers, artwork etc. – these may come in handy when establishing patterns or tracking growth and progress.

- Gather information. Read books and articles on your child's condition, attend workshops, conferences and any parent training. Get comfortable with education acronyms and jargon. Ask professionals lots of questions and don't be afraid to ask for clarification if their answers are confusing or complicated.

- Know your child's strengths and interests and share them with educators. By highlighting a struggling child's capabilities and talents you not only help professionals know your child as a whole, but you can also assist in identifying learning aids.

- Talk to other parents. Identify and join local parent support groups. If none exist, consider starting one.

- Emphasize solutions. While there are no miracle cures for your child's condition it's important to stress the positive and to help identify ways to improve your child's experience. Once appropriate programmes have been identified and agreed upon make every effort to encourage follow-through.

- Focus on the big picture. Simply put, 'don't sweat the small stuff'. Knowing the specifics of a law may be important on one level but constantly arguing technicalities can ultimately waste time and prevent positive relationships from forming. Try not to take things personally and always consider both sides of the story. Details are important but don't let them get in the way of negotiating the best experience for your child.

- Involve your child in decision making as early as you can. Remember your child has a vested interest in all that concerns them. Moreover many disabilities are a lifelong issue so mastering self-advocacy skills is one of the keys to becoming a successful adult. Resist the natural urge to pave every road for your child and respect and support your child's need to take informed academic risks.

- Don't give up. Aim for and celebrate incremental victories and accomplishments. Remember advocacy is an ongoing process!

Always keep at the back of your mind that there's no right or wrong way to be an advocate for your child. Advocacy efforts and initiatives should be individually crafted to meet your needs, your community and the particular issues, circumstances and needs within your family. Advocacy is also hard work. Even when people want to help and are willing to listen it takes lots of time and energy to change the system. But when it works – and it often does – the outcome is clearly worthwhile. You really can make a difference both for your own child and ultimately for all children who need and deserve access to appropriate and effective services.

The rest of the family also needs unwavering support. Think of a flight safety announcement: 'In case of emergency, oxygen masks will drop down in front of you. Please pull the mask down towards your face and place the mask over your mouth and nose. If you are travelling with a child, please attend to yourself first and then the child.' So too families – parents and siblings – must take care of themselves in order to have the capacity to take care of the child with special needs. I am not advocating that families should farm out the child with special needs and continue without them but time should be purposefully built into the schedule for each family member to spend time with one another or with their parents.

Chapter 34

The Child Nathan Grew and Was Strong

This year Nathan celebrates his 11th birthday. Like so many other families who have been gifted with a child with special needs Nathan's story has become our story; his journey has become our journey. What began as a tragedy has grown into something amazing. I would be lying if I said that I have enjoyed all of the conditions of the ride. There have been many times when I have felt like I have nothing left to give – when I am so exhausted at night, physically, mentally and emotionally that I fall into a dark, deep, dreamless sleep. But little by little something changed on the inside. The day I met my son, looked deep into his eyes and saw him as he was – a unique expression of God in the earth – was the day that everything changed. It didn't appear to be a big change, just a slight shift – ever so slight – and the next thing I knew I could see my son! Beyond his disabilities, past what he is not able to do. I saw him, I believe as God sees him; as a life that is valuable; as a living, breathing human being; full of potential and possibilities.

Raising Nathan

Now I see that Nathan's is a life where the only limitations are those that society or I place on him.

I believe that I was liberated from my limited view that day. Over the years I have also watched the change sweep through my whole family as we learned to see beyond Nathan's disabilities. If I was to think of one word to describe Nathan, the first that comes to mind is 'impish'. That is because he embodies a unique spirit and energy that is edgy, playful and mischievous. An endearing little scamp at heart, he takes full advantage of his 'last-child' privileges whether it is bossing around his older siblings, monopolizing the television, getting that extra piece of cake or just annoying his brother and sisters! His charm and special negotiating skills get him his own way almost every time. I would often respond to a shout from one of his siblings complaining that Nathan did so and so and would go to them to find Nathan looking straight-faced, watching TV or engaged in some other activity, while appearing not to be paying them any attention. Only a slight telltale grin tugging at the corners of his month would be the give away that he was guilty as charged!

The Child Nathan Grew
and Was Strong

Nathan has been such a blessing to our family and to those who take the time to get to know him. He has the most beautiful eyes; his paternal grandmother often refers to them as 'ackee-seed' eyes describing the contrast of the brown of his iris against the white of his cornea surrounded by enviable long lush black eyelashes. His eyes flash with life and energy and when he adds his signature 'million dollar' smile he disarms everybody and gets away with almost anything, whether at home or at school.

Our family has grown closer together because of Nathan. We all take part in his daily care. Having made the adjustment and transition we are now able to enjoy the excitement of each new achievement and the ups and downs that life with Nathan brings. We have had many good experiences, courtesy of Nathan's disabilities, including an all-inclusive trip to Disney World, Universal Studios and Sea World in Orlando for our entire family. We were also given the VIP treatment at Disney and Nathaniel's Hope Make'm Smile (Florida, USA) and countless other treats because of Nathan.

Today Nathan's development continues to be challenged not by the disability itself but by his environment.

He, and thousands of other children like him in Jamaica, continue to be challenged because they are not able to consistently access the therapies they so desperately need to help them increase their independence and improve the quality of life. He cannot access the adaptive aids, assistive technologies and special education supports that would help him in his holistic development.

It would be wrong at this point to claim that all of the emotional and psychological hurdles have been overcome because as we see Nathan entering puberty new challenges present themselves. But we are committed as a family unit to first love him unconditionally and in doing so to take special care of his complete development. We are always seeking new ways to adapt his physical environment to allow him greater independence. My next big project is to find a special educator who will work with him one on one in school and at home for the next three or so years. I don't want just a special educator, but someone who feels a call to practical ministry in this way, whether from home in Jamaica or abroad. Someone graced with the same spirit that we his family, have for him and the motivation to help him grow and thrive. I can see that there is still so much more in him that he is only just getting a chance to express and I can only imagine how frustrating that must be for him.

Nonetheless until we find such a person, we daily strive to build and encourage his self-esteem. We are not experts in these matters but have learned a thing or two. My faith has deepened as a result of this journey and I have learned to listen to and rely on my instincts. I have also gained a good team and support base along the way. But most importantly as a family we have learned to trust and rely on God, in whose eyes it is stated that Nathan is 'fearfully and wonderfully made'. We have learned to see that bit by bit each day.

Raising Nathan

Epilogue

This Gift From God

Today as I look back, Nathan's beginnings seem a distant memory. Now that there is distance I can see with much more clarity how his journey has brought many gifts and blessings into my life. While I was on my own path, with my own plans and dreams, God had other plans for why He gave me the gift of life. He had decided from before the foundation of the earth that I would bring each of my children, at the time I brought them, into the world. Even though I was being responsible, faithfully using contraceptives, he God, decided and determined that Nathan should be here. He came in spite of contraceptive.

God broke through my plans and my determination to bring this child into the world. I did everything to prevent, but God pushed past all of that and gave me this child, this gift, this Nathan. He was not my choice... he was God's choice for me, my family, my nation and the world.

So to the observer looking on, you may say, how is he a gift? You have lost so much! Yes, it is true that I gave up much – my corporate career and professional life as it was before Nathan. However I have gained much, much more– Nathan's life pushed me into becoming who I am today, as a Jamaican whose Pledge is to: *"play our part in advancing the welfare of the whole human race."* Yes, I am still a work-in progress! But much more... I am a wife, a mom, a speaker, an education consultant, a social entrepreneur, and a disability and children's advocate, and still expanding in the use of my gifts.

In 2007 I was inspired through our own struggles to form the Nathan Ebanks Foundation (NEF) with the mandate of building a bridge to support the empowerment, inclusion and participation of children with disabilities and their families in national development planning. Specifically, much of the work of the NEF has centred around creating inclusive education where children with disabilities can learn, grow and thrive alongside their non-disabled peers.

I have been blessed along the way with a closer and more knitted family, great and helpful friends, partnerships and with persons and organizations from Jamaica, the United States and more recently Canada and the United Kingdom. One outstanding individual whom I had the distinct pleasure to meet because of Nathan is Senta Greene, a dynamic, passionate and brilliant children development and inclusion specialist who resides in the United States.

I met Senta by divine appointment in 2007 when I was searching to find someone who could come to Jamaica to lead a workshop for teachers on 'Teaching Children with Disabilities in Mainstream Classrooms', so that we could equip Nathan's teachers and anyone else who was interested to teach children with learning differences. I searched the Internet until I found some-one who knew someone and although she was not available she became inspired by Nathan's story. That person referred me to someone else and five days later I met Senta. From the moment we spoke I knew that I had made a special connection. When she shared that her organization was named Full Circle, that feeling was strengthened. The proverbial icing on the cake came when I discovered that her company motto said, "To touch the heart of a child is to touch the soul of a nation." This motto came to life in the connection between Senta and me. She entered into a partnership with me because she too met Nathan and was drawn in by his charm. Since then she has been a strong partner at every stage of our journey. She has supported the work of the Nathan Ebanks Foundation since 2007, helping me to articulate, build out effect inclusion for Nathan, and through the NEF to other children in Jamaica. Together we are a determined and dedicated team of mothers and professionals committed to a cause that is greater than us. I am eternally grateful to Senta and to her family for allowing her time and space to help me to build my dream here for my son and the children of my country, Jamaica.

Two more women to whom I wish to pay tribute are Karaine Smith-Holness and Simone Fisher Sobers, these are women who have become my greatest cheerleaders and supporters. These women who took it upon themselves to create an expanded platform for the Nathan Ebanks Foundation through the Formation of the Nathan Ebanks Children Advocacy Group, a registered charity organization in New York with the mandate to raise funds to carry out the work in Jamaica on behalf of children and their families. These are women who have held up my hands when I was ready to 'throw in the towel.'

There has been many people over the years who have been drawn in by Nathan's story. This story presented me with a platform from which to do something to make a difference in the lives of others. The way I look at it, this was the push that I needed to look beyond myself and my situation and find my purpose and calling in life. Through Nathan I have learned to see his 'dis-ability' or as I love to say it, his 'this-ability' as a gift which has increased my capacity to hear what is not said and see what is not obvious. His is the gift that unlocked my potential and has helped me to personally become who I am called to be as a Jamaican... to 'play [my] part in advancing the welfare of the whole human race'.

The second stanza of our (Jamaica's) National Anthem which states

'Teach us true respect for all
stir response to duty's call

strengthen us the weak to cherish
give us vision less we perish'

came alive in me through Nathan's story. Yvonne O. Coke, in her book **Perspectives from the Jamaican MAP (Motto, Anthem, Pledge)**, stated that "As a nation we acknowledged the Eternal Fatherhood of God and Him as our source." ..., he releases the potential he has placed in us as Jamaicans, a nation born 'Out of Many One People,' to become who we are destined to become... nation-builders and world changers.' (Paraphrased).

God sends his blessings to us in many forms. We often miss them because they do not come in the way we expected, according to how we have been socialized by the world to value gifts. I am grateful for all who have played a role in Nathan's story, in my story, and my family's journey that have afforded us the blessing of seeing the gift that is Nathan, through the eyes of his Creator. And he is a good gift. A perfect gift. For me, our family, our country and the world. After all, he is fearfully and wonderfully made[1].

[1] Psalm 139 :14

References

Chapter 1

1. *Obstetrics and Gynecology.*
2. Name changed.

Chapter 2

1. Bible Gateway: *1 Thessalonians 5:18 New International Version (NIV).* Accessed 2015.
   https://www.biblegateway.com/passage/?search=1+
   Thessalonians+5:18

Chapter 3

1. Bible Gateway: *2 Samuel 11 King James Version (KJV).*
   Accessed 2015. https://www.biblegateway.com/passage/?
   search=2+Samuel+11&version=KJV

Chapter 4

1. Wikipedia: *Thoracic diaphragm.* Accessed 2014.
   http://www.wikipedia.org/wiki/Thoracic_diaphragm

2. Cherubs: *CDH Statistics*. Accessed 2015. http://www.cherubs-cdh.org/research/cdh-statistics

3. YouVersion: *Psalm 139:13-14. New International Version.* Accessed 2014. https://www.bible.com/bible/111/psa.139.13-14.niv

Chapter 10

1. MedlinePlus: *Exchange transfusion*. Accessed 2014. http://www.nlm.nih.gov/medlineplus/ency/article/002923.htm

Chapter 13

1. Babycentre: *Reflux*. Accessed 2014. http://www.babycentre.co.uk/a567208/reflux#ixzz2ysraV5bR

Chapter 14

1. University of Michigan Health System: *Developmental Delay.* Accessed 2015. http://www.med.umich.edu/yourchild/topics/devdel.htm

Chapter16

1. MedicineNet: *Definition of Peripheral vision*. Accessed 2014.

http://www.medicinenet.com/script/main/art.asp?
articlekey=10638

Chapter 17

1. Babycenter: *Cerebral Palsy: How do YOU pronounce it??*
   Accessed 2014. http://community.babycenter.com/post/
   a21981827/cerebral_palsy_how_do_you_pronounce_it
2. Healthy Children.org: *What-is-a-Child-Neurologist?*
   Accessed 2014. http://www.healthychildren.org/English/
   family-life/health-management/pediatric-specialists/Pages/
   What-is-a-Child-Neurologist.aspx
3. National Institute of Neurological Disorders and Stroke:
   NINDS Cerebral Atrophy Information Page. Accessed 2014.
   http://www.ninds.nih.gov/disorders/cerebral_atrophy/
   cerebral_atrophy.htm
4. Wikipedia: *Pachygyria.* Accessed 2014.
   http://en.wikipedia.org/wiki/Pachygyria

Chapter 18

1. Name changed.

Chapter19

1. Centre for Parent Information and Resources: *You Are Not Alone – For parents when they learn that their child has a disability by Patricia McGill Smith.* Accessed 29 March 2014. http://nichcy.org/families-community/notalone

Chapter 22

1. Mark Twain: *The Wit and Wisdom of Mark Twain: A Book of Quotations.* Dover Publications, USA. 1999.
2. Disability is Natural: *Let's Put The Person First, Not The Disability!* Accessed 2014. http://www.disabilityisnatural.com/explore/people-first-language
3. Wikipedia: *Convention on the Rights of Persons with Disabilities.* Accessed 2014. http://en.wikipedia.org/wiki/Convention_on_the_Rights_of_Persons_with_Disabilities

Chapter 23

1. Disabled World: *Famous People with Cerebral Palsy.* Accessed 2015. http://www.disabled-world.com/artman/publish/cp-famous.shtml
2. Stephen Hawking: *The Official Website.* Accessed 2015. http://www.hawking.org.uk/
3. Wikipedia: *Cerebral Palsy.* Accessed 2014.

http://en.wikipedia.org/wiki/Cerebral_palsy

4. MyChild: *Cause of Cerebral Palsy*. Accessed 2014.
http://cerebralpalsy.org/about-cerebral-palsy/cause/

5. Cerebral Palsy.org: *Signs and Symptoms*. Accessed 2015.
http://cerebralpalsy.org/about-cerebral-palsy/sign-and-symptoms/

Chapter 24

1. Modesta Pousada, Noemí Guillamón, Eulàlia Hernández-Encuentra et al. (2013). Journal of Developmental and Physical Disabilities 25(5): *Impact of caring for a child with cerebral palsy on the quality of life of parents: a systematic review of the literature*, ps.545–577.

Chapter 25

1. National Human Genome Research Institute: *Learning About Velocardiofacial Syndrome*. Accessed 2015.
https://www.genome.gov/25521139

2. Wikipedia: *Accessibility*. Accessed 2015.
http://en.wikipedia.org/wiki/Accessibility

Chapter28

1. MedicineNet.com: Cerebral Palsy by Norberto Alvarez.
   Accessed 2014.
   http://www.medicinenet.com/cerebral_palsy/page5.htm
2. HealthCentral: Failure to Thrive by Neil K. Kaneshiro. Accessed
   2014. http://www.healthcentral.com/ency/408/000991.html

Chapter 32

1. MOVE International assessment question.

Epilogue

1. Jamaican Information Service: National Pledge. Accessed 2015.
   http://jis.gov.jm/information/anthem-pledge/

About the Author

Christine Staple-Ebanks is the Founder and President of the Nathan Ebanks Foundation, a not-for-profit organization established in Jamaica which works for the inclusion, empowerment and participation of children with disabilities. In 2010, she co-founded the Nathan Ebanks Children Advocacy Group a not-for-profit (501c3) organization established in New York, USA, to render assistance to children inclusively (with and without disabilities).

A graduate of the St. Andrew High School for Girls, University of Technology and the University of the West Indies in Jamaica, Christine has more than 28 years of experience in senior positions in private and public sector organizations including more than ten years as a disability-inclusive advocate. Her advocacy work began in 2004, following the diagnosis of her fourth child, Nathan, with cerebral palsy. She switched careers to embark on a new path as a social entrepreneur, establishing the organizations to bridge the gap for information and support to children with disabilities and their families in Jamaica.

Since that time, Christine has worked tirelessly in the education and disability sectors in Jamaica, representing the issues in various national media. Her work spans capacity building and intervention for parents, teachers and policy-makers. She has worked at the early childhood, primary and secondary levels, has organized dozens of special education conferences, disability related and professional development workshops. She has served on several local and national boards and committees, including the National Disability Advisory Board. She is a frequent speaker, conference and workshop presenter, and her work has been featured in local newspapers.

Christine and her husband Robert have been married for nearly 20 years and live in Kingston, Jamaica with their four children.

Join the Raising Nathan Community to continue the discussion at *www.facebook.com/Raisingnathan* or *www.raisingnathan.com*

Christine Staple-Ebanks is donating a part of her income from this book to the Nathan Ebanks Foundation, a non-profit organization which provides programmes to support the development of children with disabilities in Jamaica.

Jamaican National Anthem

Eternal Father bless our land,
Guard us with Thy Mighty Hand,
Keep us free from evil powers,
Be our light through countless hours.
To our Leaders, Great Defender,
Grant true wisdom from above.
Justice, Truth be ours forever,
Jamaica, Land we love.
Jamaica, Jamaica, Jamaica land we love.

Teach us true respect for all,
Stir response to duty's call,
Strengthen us the weak to cherish,
Give us vision lest we perish.
Knowledge send us Heavenly Father,
Grant true wisdom from above.
Justice, Truth be ours forever,
Jamaica, land we love.
Jamaica, Jamaica, Jamaica land we love.

Jamaican National Pledge

Before God and all mankind, I pledge the love and
loyalty of my heart, the wisdom and courage of my
mind, the strength and vigour of my body in the service
of my fellow citizens; I promise to stand up for Justice,
Brotherhood and Peace, to work diligently and creatively,
to think generously and honestly, so that Jamaica may,
under God, increase in beauty, fellowship and prosperity,
and play her part in advancing the welfare of the
whole human race.

Jamaican Motto

Out of Many One People.

Nathan Ebanks Foundation
http://nefjamaica.org

The Nathan Ebanks Foundation (NEF) was founded in 2007 by Christine Staple Ebanks and her husband Robert Ebanks, in honour of their son who at the age of nine months, was diagnosed with cerebral palsy.

The Foundation is the product of the collective vision of this family's experience in raising a child with disabilities, and is established on the mission to ensure that all children, with disabilities and special needs, are included, empowered and supported to access and participate in holistic development –
education, intellectual, emotional, social, physical, artistic, creative and spiritual – to release their full potential.

Nathan Ebanks Foundation
6 Montgomery Road, P.O. Box 2334,
Kingston 8, Jamaica
(+876) 857-4425 or (+876) 632-7835
info@nefjamaica.org

Nathan Ebanks Children Advocacy Group Inc.
http://www.nefjamaica.org/index.php/pages/
nathan-ebanks-children-advocacy-group

The Nathan Ebanks Children Advocacy Group Inc. (NECAG) is a not-for-profit charitable 501(c)(3) organization built on the principles of love, service and philanthropy; and has been established to render assistance to children inclusively (children with and without disabilities) in the areas of:

Education
Inclusive Development
Holistic Development
Healthcare, and
Economic Development

The NECAG works with and through the Nathan Ebanks Foundation and stakeholders to bring about change in the lives of children and their families, particularly those who are marginalized, socially and economically excluded, with disabilities/special needs and others who are in need. By partnering and contributing to the NECAG you have the ability to give an education to those who have none; to provide much needed intervention and medical care to children with disabilities, children at risk and children with special needs.

The Nathan Ebanks Children Advocacy Group Inc. 170-24 130th Avenue, Apt. #2G, Jamaica NY 11434 / P.O. Box 341033, Jamaica New York, 11434

We appreciate and salute our sponsors and supporters.

Made in the USA
Middletown, DE
24 April 2016